HOW TO TALK TO ANYONE

Learn How To Improve Communication Skills And Talk To Women, Men, In Public, At Work At Anytime And Anywhere With Confidence, Increase Your Self-Esteem, Manage Shyness

Mind Change Academy

Sommario

3

*** BONUS 1 ***

As a way of expressing my gratitude for your purchase, I am offering you a complimentary report that is only available to readers of this book.

With EMOTIONAL DIARY you'll discover a printable reference journal of rules to know how to manage your emotions.

Writing all the emotions you feel is the first step to see their effect on your life, to understand them and finally manage them to live a more peaceful life.

Everything you need to get started with EMOTIONAL DIARY is to download your free diary.

Click this link to free download

https://dl.bookfunnel.com/qx1qtousl6

Meditation Music

We have created a YouTube channel to give you the opportunity to listen to relaxing music to meditate, relax, study, work and sleep better.
The numerous beneficial effects of music on the human being have been confirmed by many scientific researches around the world. Listening to it increases the production of serotonin (a natural antidepressant), reduces the secretion of stress hormones (cortisol) and stimulates the production of beta-endorphins (analgesics produced by the body), acting as a real antidote against states of anxiety, insomnia and psychophysical fatigue.

Meditation music, for example, is a very effective tool for combating stress, easing tensions, alleviating the rhythms of modern life and bringing general well-being.

It also has a positive effect on feelings of depression, anxiety or loneliness, but a close relationship between music, cognitive processes and human mood has also been demonstrated.

These are just some of the benefits you can gain from listening to relaxing music for meditation:
- Relief from stress and anxiety
- Improves the quality of rest and sleep by calming the nerves and diverting attention from a noisy brain.
- Increases concentration and memory capacity
- Improves physical health by helping your body heal and rest
- Rebalances heart and respiratory function
- Reduces blood pressure levels
- Improves blood oxygenation through deep breathing
- Activates energy and vitality levels

6

- Helps with positive thinking
- Increases self-awareness
- Stimulates creativity
- Instils self-esteem

YOUTUBE https://bit.ly/3dyv5u7

FACEBOOK **_https://bit.ly/3SWKlRB_**

Introduction

Hello there! How've you been? Exhausted? It's understandable. Failing to effectively get your point across in communication, particularly in the relationships we have to deal with daily such as family, friends or even co-workers can make you feel drained.

After all, if you have to explain yourself twenty million times, who wouldn't be annoyed, right? Do you hear that little voice inside your head, the one that keeps agreeing with everything you just read—quite the antagonizer isn't it?

It feels an awful lot like you're mad at the people around you, doesn't it? It's as if their misunderstanding and failing to fall in line is a reflection on who they are as people.

Well, be that as it may, have you ever wondered if there is something you could fix in terms of how you are communicating?

Think about it—have you been having trouble communicating? Have you ever felt like what you are saying and what you mean aren't really the same, and you haven't been coming across well?

Yes?

Have you ever wondered why?

The lack of dynamic communication at work and home is extremely damaging to both careers and healthy family life. This is because feeling frustrated or unheard when dealing with people you engage with daily is basically the highway to a mental breakdown. As human beings, we need to know that what we do matters, and we need to feel respected and appreciated. And the only way to ensure that, is by working on our communication skills, so we are better equipped to understand and deal with one another.

Are you looking for ways to improve your communication skills, even when discussing difficult topics such as politics, race, or gender? If so, this article on Effective Communication will provide you with five essential tips and exercises to help you communicate more effectively in this divided world.

With modern day communication becoming more and more difficult, with so many divisive issues such as race and religious freedom being pushed to the forefront, it's understandable that people with different views would have a tough time finding common ground from where they can respectfully disagree. But it's not impossible!

And we are here to walk you through exactly how to do this!

Ready?

It's okay; you don't have to be—for now, just listen.

When you are communicating, or when you are being communicated with, there are five key concepts that will determine how effective this communication is going to be. They are often called the five Core Concepts of Communication and are listening, delivery, empathy, honesty, and winning. Every single one of these topics has the unique ability to help change minds and attitudes when properly applied.

You know what that means, right?

It means no more fights at the dinner table or pulling your hair out over what your boss has been saying. Once you've gone through this book and actively applied each of these five techniques, you'll be ready to take on the world—literally!

So, what do you say?

Are you ready now?

Awesome! Keep reading; we got you!

The Basics of Communication

Meaning, Concept and Process of Communication

Effective communication is generally a business term, and it's something that is generally used to ensure that a complete, coherent form of communication is being undertaken, and in such a manner that the person you are communicating with understands the message conveyed in the way in which the communicator intended it to be understood.

Pretty easy, right?

What you just did is the single most complicated thing mankind has ever done. In fact, only the human race is capable of full communication, to the extent of ensuring that the message we deliver is "conveyed in the manner in which the communicator intended it to be understood".

Generally, we turn to the seven C's of communication. Correctness, whereby you ensure that the information you are delivering is correct and accurate. Clarity makes sure you aren't complicating things, remember to stay focused and stick to one issue. The best way to do that is to ensure you are Concise, cover what needs to be covered without embellishment, don't create too much build up just get in there, and get to the point. Having said that, it is equally important that you keep an eye out to ensure that the message being sent is Complete. And then in quick succession, you have Consideration, Concreteness, and Courtesy. Your concreteness comes from the authenticity of what you are saying, and to finish off, there is a courtesy which is the polish on top that keeps the audience happy and willing to listen.

But all of this is about the message we are dealing with—how we deliver this message is a whole other issue.

So, let's get straight to it, shall we?

Mindset and Approach

We all share an internal desire to relate to the world around us. Imagine for a moment, if you could no longer communicate and nobody was able to understand anything that you're trying to tell them. Life would be an unending series of frustrations on your part, mostly. Remove this ability and suddenly life becomes a struggle when nobody can understand your needs and vice versa.

Before you can begin successfully improving your ability to communicate with the people around you, there's something that you need to do first. Your ability to interact with others is going to stem from the experiences you have had in the past, and since experience can be the most effective teacher or all, the experiences of the past are going to impact your communicative ability moving forward. If you can't understand yourself at the most basic level, you can't expect others around you to understand who you are and what you need either.

Effective communication begins with you, and the first place to start is through developing a level of self-awareness about yourself. The ability to reflect on your internal experiences and make sense out of it allows you to accurately process your emotions. This will enable you to determine just how much far your thoughts and emotions are influencing your communication process and the way they affect your nonverbal cues. If you were trying to have a professional conversation but you were in a bad mood over something that happened earlier, having those feelings still coursing through your system is going to negatively impact the conversation you're now trying to have. Your tone might sound harsher than you think, or the annoyance and stress you're feeling might be reflected on in the slight frown between your brows or the downward curve of your mouth. Little signals will be picked up on by the receiving party. Understanding yourself better with the right level of self-awareness might have made you realize that perhaps you were not in the right frame of mind for an effective conversation, and you could have then made the necessary arrangements to postpone it to a better time, or you could have given yourself time to prepare beforehand.

For an effective conversation to take place, emotions must be regulated, and you cannot regulate your emotions without self-awareness. Why is it so important for emotions to be regulated during the communication process? Because our emotions influence our speech and thought process. When you're feeling particularly angry, those emotions might make you perceive the message you're receiving in a different way. What was meant as an innocent remark suddenly gets taken out of context and an argument ensues? A situation that could have easily been avoided if you understood yourself to know that perhaps you were letting your emotions cloud your judgment. An awareness that could have led you to react very differently and produced an entirely different outcome.

To a certain extent, being able to communicate effectively involves emotional intelligence. The five key abilities that comprise emotional intelligence (empathy, social skills, self-awareness, self-regulation, and motivation) are also the essential skills that allow you to converse with almost anyone in a great way. Understanding yourself and managing your emotions gives you the necessary skills to recognise your own emotions, capacities and then regulate the correct behaviour to reach the most desirable result. Empathy and social skills help you connect beyond more than just the surface with the person you're talking to. To be able to put yourself in their shoes, see what they see, feel what they feel, that gives you the valuable insight you need to tailor your messages accordingly. Last but not least, motivation gives you the determination and the drive that you need to stay focused on the bigger picture, to stay focused on why you're having this conversation and what message it is you're trying to deliver.

Without emotional intelligence, making the necessary connection you need with your audience in order to be able to engage them effectively becomes increasingly more difficult. Self-awareness is such a vital part of the communication process and here's an example of why. There will be some people who, despite your best efforts, will prove to be almost impossible to communicate effectively with. You might have family members with whom you can't see eye-to-eye with, no matter how hard you try. You may have colleagues at work with whom you're constantly butting heads with, even though you're trying to best communicate with them to the best of your abilities. As challenging as these people might be, you still have to interact with them, it's unavoidable. Self-awareness can be a big help in this instance.

When you know what your strengths are, you can use them to your advantage in the moments when you need to communicate with these challenging individuals. Knowing your own strengths and weaknesses is crucial because once you know the warning signs within yourself, you can then mitigate the potential for arguments to ensue.

The Self-Communication Principle (Intrapersonal Communication)

Before you begin any kind of important speech, you need to be confident about the content you're going to deliver. This process is called intrapersonal communication, and it involves having a conversation with yourself. Most people don't realize it, but we already have internal dialogues with ourselves all the time. Whether you're doing it consciously or not, the scenarios you play in your mind, the conversations you imagine yourself having, that's all part of the intrapersonal communication that's going on.

The internal monologues we run in our minds are just as important as the external conversations that take place. Communicating with ourselves is an important tool that helps build both our self-perception and self-esteem. The self-talk you have with yourself affects your emotional and mental wellbeing more than you realize. The next time an internal dialogue is happening, tune in and pay close attention to what you are telling yourself. Is the self-communication that's taking place positive? Or does it slant more towards the negative? The latter, of course, is going to drain you of your motivation and your energy levels, robbing you of your self-esteem and confidence in the process if you're constantly focused on your flaws and all the things you can't do. Positive self-talk, on the other hand, can have the complete opposite effect, empowering you and boosting your confidence and self-esteem levels, making you feel like you can conquer any obstacle that comes your way.

Visualization is a strong part of the self-communication principle. Athletes, motivational speakers, and successful individuals rely on visualization to mentally prepare themselves for the performance ahead. Athletes visualize themselves giving their best performance before they head into the game. Motivational speakers imagine themselves in front of a crowd, inspiring the crowd to live their best lives. Successful people visualize themselves achieving their goals. You are now going to apply this same visualization technique by picturing in your mind the way you want a conversation to go before you have it.

Type of Person: Visual, Kinesthetic and Hearing

When we communicate, we typically employ expressions like "It is clear to me," "I feel it," or "It sounds great" to express similar concepts. Nevertheless, these words and phrases can signify different senses; sight, feeling, and hearing. We often rely on just one of these senses when we talk. For instance, if somebody is inclined to be more visually oriented, they may use terms such as "clear," "simple," "I can see," or "a perspective." In contrast, someone who uses more of a sense of feeling may say phrases like "I feel," "hard," "hold," "smoothly," and "touch."3

When speaking, a person may utilize sensory perceptions to convey their message, which can be categorized into three main types: visual, auditory, and kinesthetic:

- Visual – People who rely a lot on their sense of sight typically communicate with phrases like "I can see it clearly", "I get what you mean", "your future looks promising" and words like "view", "image", "hue", "foggy", "plain", "forecast", "appear" or "vantage point". They may also use terms related to vision such as "small", "faint", "brown", "rectangular" and so on.

- Auditory – Those who rely more heavily on their auditory senses tend to use language related to sound, such as "I hear you," "she scratched the floor," "his voice was sharp," and "I am listening to you," as well as words like "listen," "talk," "discuss," "hear," "sound," "call," etc. They also often use terms related to sound to describe shapes, like "loud," "noisy," "beeping," "ticking," etc.
- Kinesthetic – People with a kinesthetic sensory perception often use language associated with emotions or physical sensations when they communicate, such as "I think that's the best way to do it," "My feelings don't agree with this," "She was very inviting," "I get that," "I can't understand that," or "I'm worried about that," as well as words like "touch," "feel," "scared," "fear," "warm," "cold," "rough," "smooth," "wet," and so on.

It is important to take note of these details and adapt your speech accordingly. To help with this, practice creating sentences that contain elements from each of the five senses. This will make it easier to slip them into real conversations. Test out one of the techniques during your next conversation and then try another one to see how it works for you.

By focusing on one aspect at a time, you can train your mind to recognize what the other person is saying more easily. This way, you can gradually acquire the skill and be able to use it without thinking. With this improved communication ability, you will be able to adjust your behavior in various situations. Additionally, I will inform you about various verbal patterns and forms of thought, and how to identify and take advantage of them.

It is essential to be alert and cautious when conversing and listening to others. Although I made a commitment to listen to others intently some time ago, I often find myself not paying close attention to the words being said and slipping into autopilot mode, thus losing sight of my objectives in the exchange.

Over time I was able to focus on and pay attention to what the other person was saying, becoming aware of their beliefs, values, experiences, and the words and phrases that evoked sensory responses. It's important to remember that this is a skill that can be learned and when used properly, can open up many possibilities. Start using it in your life today!

The Levels of Communication Verbal & Non-Verbal

Verbal Communication

Speech is what most people think about when the word communication is mentioned.

We use our speech so much in communicating with other people that we have tens of thousands of words for different things.

The English alphabet alone has twenty-six different letters representing particular sounds used in English speech. In other cultures, like Chinese and Japanese, their "alphabet" is more syllabic with hundreds of symbols representing particular things. In some African dialects, there's even a tongue click represented in English as an exclamation mark.

Given the complexity of speech and all of its components, it's our most powerful and versatile communication tool. Let's discuss each of these components, then move on to the nonverbal elements of communication.

Language

The first component I want to discuss is language because one thing can have different terms used to describe it among the thousands of different languages and dialects in the world.

If you're someone who wants to communicate effectively with someone, you first have to make sure that you speak the same language.

If you only know English like most Americans, then you're okay if you're only ever around people who speak English. However, when you're suddenly in a situation where you're to talk to someone who doesn't know English, then you're automatically placed at a huge disadvantage.

In my job as a company representative, I get exposed to people who speak different languages, but the most common language I encounter is Latin American Spanish.

I never understood Spanish back when I was young, and growing up in California, there were a lot of kids who spoke both Spanish and English, and their parents sometimes only spoke Spanish.

I remember hanging out with at my friend's house after school one time, and his grandma approached me telling me something in Spanish, and I couldn't make out what she was telling me, so I called my friend over. He then translated for me, telling me that his grandma was asking if I was hungry and wanted some tamales. I said I wasn't hungry, but I would love to try their tamales, which my friend translated back to his grandma.

If I knew how to speak Spanish, I wouldn't have been confused about what his grandma was saying, and I wouldn't have needed to call him over to translate for me.

21

It was when I realized that I needed to learn Spanish because I didn't want to be confused like that again. I started hanging out at that friend's house more often and gradually picked up on their language.

Until now, I can understand Spanish very well, although my accent is still funny according to that same friend, who I still hang out with a lot and go on hikes with monthly.

If you're in an area with people who speak a different language, it would be to your advantage to learn to speak their language.

That way you don't miss out on anything and also sometimes it's fun to listen to people talk when they think that you don't understand them.

Also, learning to speak a different language makes you smarter and helps you avoid little mishaps that happen because of things getting lost in translation.

Your Vocabulary

How many words do you know? It's kind of hard to count because each of us knows hundreds of different words we use in conversations.

How about your spelling? Are you a good speller, or do you often find yourself being confused about how something is spelled? Do you use "night," or do you spell it "nite"? Do you know the difference between "you're" and "your," or do you use "your" interchangeably?

The way you spell matters a lot only if you do a lot of writing, but if you're only talking most of the time, then you might not have to worry too much, although you might still want to improve on your spelling.

Essentially, your vocabulary is the number of words you know. It matters because the type of conversations you hold and the level of intelligence you display largely depends on the type of words you use in talking to someone.

For example, if you're not a big gamer and you start talking to someone who is into gaming a lot, you'll start hearing things like "fps" and a lot of gaming jargon that I myself do not understand.

I have a friend who is heavy into games, and aside from simply playing, he makes it a hobby to find bugs in the games that he can exploit to perform things that aren't even supposed to be possible in the game officially.

When I talk to him, sometimes I don't get the things he's trying to tell me, and I always find myself asking for clarification. Eventually, he got annoyed by my clarification requests that he learned to dumb things down for me.

The kind of words you use in speaking to someone can really define you in their heads.

When I took a marketing class, we were taught to use simple words that a ten-year-old can clearly understand because most people don't use complicated words in everyday speech. If you start using deep words, then a lot of what you're trying to say in your marketing campaigns could simply fly over people's heads.

So basically, we were taught to keep our words light and easy to understand. That's essentially what you should do as well. You have to keep your words at a level where the person you're talking to is not getting confused.

Grammar

Grammar refers to the way your words are organized. You can be the most eloquent person out there knowing so many complicated words. You can also know every possible language out there. But, if your grammar is terrible, then your message won't be sent as clearly as you want it.

Now, most adults develop grammar naturally. The way most people normally speak in their native tongue is the correct grammar. The problem usually arises when you speak a different language.

For example, in English, you say, "I understand Japanese," but in Japanese, the grammar structure is "Watashi-wa Nihongo-ga Wakarimas" or in literal English, "I Japanese understand". If you're a native English speaker and you speak Japanese to a Japanese person, you might speak it in a way that follows the English grammar structure instead of their native grammar structure.

If you want to communicate effectively, you have to understand the grammar rules very well, and you have to structure your words and sentences in a way that doesn't muddle the message you're trying to relay.

Your Tone

Now that we're done with the actual words themselves let's go to the other stuff about the way you speak that gives context to what you're saying because really, there's a lot more to what you're saying aside from the words you use and one big part of it is the tone of your voice when you are speaking.

Here's how important your tone is. As an example, I want you to imagine the following:

24

Your mother yelling your first name.

Your lover gently speaking your first name.

Your friend casually calling you by the first name.

In each case, the same word is used, which is your first name. But, each is said in a different tone, and each case means a different thing than the others.

That's how effective tone is when you use it. The mere tone of your voice can be a message in itself. It indicates your mood and your intent.

Even if you use the nicest words you can find in your entire vocabulary and use the best, most eloquent grammar; it's still not going to come across as something good if your tone indicates hostility because you're yelling and the way you speak is pointed.

At the same time, even if you use the most hostile, offensive words you have and even threaten violence, the effect won't be as intimidating if you say it in monotone. I was actually going to say, "if you use a soft tone," but sometimes, violent threats can sound even scarier if spoken in a soft voice.

Your tone can easily change the context of your statements, so you have to understand how your tone of voice works and what the appropriate tone is for every message you want to send.

Your Speed

Aside from the tone of your voice, other indicators also exist, such as the speed of your speech.

Of course, there are times when you have to control the speed of your speech like when you're speaking to someone who is hard of hearing. In that case, you normally have to speak a little slower for the other person to be able to hear each word you are saying properly.

When you're in a hurry then, of course, you have to speak a little quicker than usual, so you can finish delivering the message in the short time you have to deliver it.

For the most part, however, when you don't consciously control the speed of your speech, it usually indicates your energy.

When you speak very fast, to the listener, it could indicate high energy. It's when you're excited or agitated. On the other hand, when you speak very slowly, then the listener might take it as a lack of enthusiasm on your part.

Sometimes, people even associate slow speech with a low level of intelligence because somehow, it seems like it takes someone who speaks slow, a little more time to process their own words.

So the speed you use when talking to people is also very important, and you need to be aware of it and control it as much as you can.

Your Volume

Your volume can say a lot, too, about the nature of the message you're trying to tell someone.

If you've ever whispered to someone's ear, then you know that you probably had to speak it softly to avoid being overheard by others. On the other hand, when you're watching a game, you're probably yelling loudly at the players because you want them to hear your frustration and tell them what they should be doing.

So basically, the volume of your voice could indicate how much you want to be heard.

I remember an uncle of mine who has hearing problems. He always yells his words because well, he can't hear himself speak, and he forgets that other people can hear fine, so when he can't hear himself, he thinks other people can't hear him as well. So, he speaks loudly to hear himself speak and assure himself that the people he is speaking to can hear him as well.

Other than wanting to be heard, your volume can also indicate your confidence levels.

Usually, a shy person speaks softly because they're afraid of being heard and humiliated. On the other hand, a person who is self-assured may speak a little louder because they want to be clearly heard.

Nonverbal Communication

Now that you know the components of verbal communication and why each of them should matter to you, we'll discuss the components of nonverbal communication because communication is not just about what you are saying. It's also about what you are doing because everything you do sends a message, and as someone who wants to project charisma, you need to be aware of these as well and be able to master and control nonverbal communication as well.

Before we proceed to discuss the components of nonverbal communication, let me tell you the story of a man named Jeremiah Denton.

Back in the Vietnam war, he was captured and forced to go on a propaganda video in 1966.

While the video was being shot, he pretended to be irritated with the lighting used during filming and blinked while talking during the video. As it turned out, his blinking was a message in morse code saying "torture."

27

Since then, every video being sent out by kidnap victims, figures like terrorists and criminals, and politicians are thoroughly analyzed for hidden messages before anything else is done with them, like broadcasting on TV, for example.

Also, if you've ever seen the show Lie To Me, the premise is how they analyze nonverbal cues, which then becomes clues to solving crimes or resolving conflicts in the episodes. It's a TV show, but it doesn't mean that the concept of reading nonverbal cues is all fiction. It's actually being actively practiced.

As I said, your nonverbal cues also send a message, and you need to be a master of it as well and not just be reliant on verbal communication.

Proxemics

In simple terms, proxemics is the study of how you use space in social interactions. Basically, what it means is that the distance between you and another person and where you are relative to the things around you and the people you interact with have meanings.

I know it can still be a bit confusing, but I'm sure it will be a bit clearer once I go into further detail.

First, have you heard of the term "personal space"?

If you haven't or if you've heard it used but didn't fully understand what it means, then let me explain.

According to experts, particularly Edward T. Hall, in his book The Hidden Dimension, we have four different zones determined by our preferred distance when it comes to other people. I'm going to discuss it next, starting from the outer zone, down to the innermost zone.

First is the public zone, which is the outermost zone, and it's said to be between twelve to twenty-five feet or more.

In this zone, there's no physical or even eye contact. Think about when you shop at the department store. You try to keep a distance from the other shoppers as much as possible, right? It's because you don't know them, and you're probably not even remotely interested in them.

The second zone is called the social zone, and it's anywhere from four to twelve feet away from you.

Again, think of shopping at the department store. Imagine meeting an acquaintance, maybe someone who you've seen at work a few times, and you want to say "Hi". Or, maybe you saw someone you found interesting or is standing at a product you're curious about, and you want to ask for their opinion about the product. You get close to them, but not too close, right?

You just get close enough for them to hear you talk to them, but you keep a safe distance where they can't just reach you without you noticing or being able to react.

The third zone is called the personal zone, which is about eighteen inches to four feet from you.

This is the zone where you keep your friends and other people you're comfortable with, like certain family members. It's close enough to talk and to shake hands.

When you see a friend the department store, you approach them and even pat them in the back or shoulder for them to notice you if you were coming from behind.

The fourth zone is called the intimate zone, and it's from eighteen inches to direct contact.

It's usually where you keep the people you really care about and are really comfortable with, like your really close friends, significant other, or your children.

When you see them in the department store, you're comfortable enough to hug them or kiss them.

So, basically, the amount of distance you place between you and another person could be interpreted as your level of comfort and intimacy with them.

When you stand too far from a person, then they might take it as you not being comfortable around them.

In addition to the different zones, there's also your eye level in relation to another person, or how high you are positioned from the other person.

For example, you might get intimidated by someone who is far taller than you or when you're sitting, and they're standing in front of you while talking to you.

Usually, a higher position indicates power over the person in a lower position. If you've seen the Star Wars prequels or at least have seen the meme where Obi-Wan Kenobi tells Anakin Skywalker that he has the higher ground and presumes that he has a greater advantage, it's like that.

That's why politicians and other people giving speeches are usually positioned higher using a stage or a podium. Someone giving a speech on a stage is going to be taken more seriously than someone who gives a speech on the ground floor. Of course, there are practicality issues that have to be considered, so it's not always true.

However, according to studies done in the medical field, in particular, doctor-patient relationships are significantly better when the doctor levels with the patient by stooping or sitting down than when they stand up and tower over a patient lying down in a hospital bed.

Introduction to Emotional Intelligence

Goleman has made popular the concept of emotional intelligence that defines as the ability to understand and manage our emotions and those of those around us, in the most convenient and satisfactory way.

He believes that emotional intelligence is based on the ability to communicate effectively with ourselves and with others and that these skills are not something innate but learned, so we can always improve them.

When talking about emotions, it refers to attitudes (that is, beliefs loaded with emotions that predispose us to act in a manner consistent with them), and automatic reactions (not voluntary or conscious) with emotional content.

According to Goleman, people with emotional intelligence have the following characteristics:

- They understand their own and others' emotions, desires and needs, and act wisely based on them.
- They properly manage their feelings and those of others and tolerate tensions well.
- They are independent, self-confident, sociable, outgoing, cheerful and balanced.
- Their emotional life is rich and appropriate, and when they fall into an adverse mood, they know how to get out of it easily, without getting caught in their negative emotions.
- They tend to maintain an optimistic view of things and feel comfortable with themselves, with their peers and with the kind of life they lead.

31

- They express their feelings properly, without surrendering to emotional outbursts that they would later have to regret.

Goleman differentiates between intrapersonal and interpersonal emotional intelligence. The first is very similar to self-esteem, while the second is closely related to HH SS, as we will see in the next two sections.

Intrapersonal Emotional Intelligence

Goleman describes intrapersonal emotional intelligence in a manner similar to what we understand by self-esteem, although focusing on feelings. He believes that an important aspect of intrapersonal emotional intelligence is the ability to communicate effectively with ourselves; that is, to perceive, organize and remember our experiences, thoughts, and feelings in the ways that are best for us.

This intrapersonal communication is essential to control our emotions, adapt them to the moment or the situation, stop being slaves of them, and be better able to face optimally any setback, without altering ourselves more conveniently.

This emotional self-control does not consist in repressing emotions, but in keeping them in balance, since each emotion has its own function and its adaptive value, provided that it does not become excessive or does not "overflow."

Emotional balance is the desirable alternative to two undesirable opposing attitudes, consisting of 1) repressing or denying our emotions - which would make us inhibited - or, 2) letting ourselves be carried away by emotional excesses such as a self-destructive crush or extreme anger.

The search for emotional well-being is a constant effort in the life of any person, although many times we are not aware of it. Thus, for example, many of the daily activities,

32

such as watching television, going out with friends, etc., are aimed at reducing our negative emotions and increasing positive emotions.

Interpersonal Emotional Intelligence

Goleman believes that interpersonal emotional intelligence is the ability to relate effectively to our emotions and those of others, in the field of interpersonal relationships. It includes being able to:

- Adequately express our emotions verbally and nonverbally, taking into account their impact on other people's emotions.
- Help others experience positive emotions and reduce the negative ones (e.g., anger).
- Get interpersonal relationships to help us achieve our goals, realize our desires and experience as many positive emotions as possible.
- Reduce the negative emotions that interpersonal conflicts can cause us.

For Goleman, a key factor in interpersonal emotional intelligence is empathy, which he defines as the ability to understand the feelings of others and put ourselves in the place of the other. Given its importance in the HH SS, we dedicate the following section to it.

Effective Oral Communication

The First Rule of Conversation: Listen

A good speaker is someone who is also an excellent listener. Effective communication is as much about developing your listening skills as your speaking skills.

Don't interrupt when a person is speaking. Interrupting a person can send a wrong message. It tells the other person that you are more important than them or that what they are saying is not as exciting as what you are saying. It can also convey you don't care about what the other thinks or feels, or that you don't have time to hear their opinion/take on a matter.

Isn't it amazing how some people turn a regular conversation into a contest that must be won? It isn't always about saying the best lines or having the last word. Some people don't believe in cooperating or collaborating but view everything as a competition. Instead of listening to other people, they will be thinking about what to say or framing their sentences when the other person is talking. They look to reply not to understand.

If you don't understand a thing, ask the speaker to go over it again. However, don't interrupt immediately. Wait for the speaker to pause. Once the speaker pauses, you can say something such as, "Wait a second, please. I didn't get what you just said about..." Offer acknowledgments to show you are keenly listening to the person. It can be anything from verbal nods to "hm" and "ah." The idea is to offer the speaker some clue that you are not just listening to him or her but also absorbing what they are saying.

One of the best acknowledgment tips is to reflect on the speaker's emotions or feelings by paraphrasing or validating what they said. "It must have been a terrible situation for you" or "You must be so happy!" or "I understand you are disturbed" are typical examples of acknowledging the speaker's feelings. Paraphrasing also works well. So what you are trying to say is……". This tells the speaker that you have been listening to them all along.

Keep an open mind and listen to the other person without succumbing to the temptation of judging and criticizing them. Sometimes, we feel an irresistible urge to throw in our two cents or give our opinion/suggestion about something as a person is peaking. At times what they say is even alarming! However, get out of the habit of mentally rating or judging what they are saying and just listen to them. Sometimes, all people want when they are speaking is a listening ear. They've probably already figured out what they want to do.

Unless the person is actively seeking your opinion or suggestions, avoid sharing it. Listen without making conclusions. Language is only a representation of the person's feelings and thoughts. You really don't know what is happening in a person's mind. Listen to them carefully to figure it out. Again, avoid being a sentence grabber. This is especially true when you are communicating with a person you know intimately. The urge to finish what they started saying is high. The speaker is led by his own train of thoughts, and you really don't know where it is headed. The person wants you to hear them not speak for them or throw in your two cents.

Empathy is crucial when it comes to being a good listener. Try and feel the emotions of a person while they are speaking, and express the same through facial expressions. For example, if the person is expressing sadness, your facial expressions should convey to him or her that you feel their sadness. This makes you come across as a concerned, empathetic and effective speaker.

Empathy is the cornerstone of active listening. Place yourself in the other person's shoes and feel the emotions and feelings the other person is undergoing at that moment. It paves the way for better communication. When the speaker realizes you are keenly listening to them and feeling their emotions, they are likelier to share more.

As a listener, you must be attentive yet relaxed. You don't have to keep staring at the person while he or she is talking. Look away occasionally, and then get back to the speaker. Stay attentive though. Nothing irks a speaker more than an inattentive listener! Be mentally present and give full attention to what the speaker is saying. Screen out disturbances like electronic gadgets and background noises. Again, the biggest distractions unknowingly come from within us. We are likelier to be distracted by our own thoughts, biases, and feelings.

Ask questions only to get a better understanding of what the person is trying to say and do not interrupt the flow of what the speaker is trying to communicate. Let's take an example. Say a co-worker Jill is telling you about a recent all girls trip she took to Europe. She's talking animatedly and excitedly about all the things she enjoyed there. In the course of her conversation, she mentions the name of a common friend Rose who was also with her on the trip. You jump in faster than you can say "Jill" and ask about Rose. "Oh, I haven't heard anything about her for a while, though last I heard was she was divorcing her abusive husband". Then the conversation shifts towards poor Rose, her unfortunate custody battle, the well-being of her children, domestic violence and family laws and more. Now, everything regarding Europe and Jill's holiday fades into oblivion.

Typically, this happens all the time. A person starts on one note, and the listener in his or zest for asking questions veers the topic in an entirely different direction. If as a speaker you notice that you've taken the subject elsewhere, take responsibility of bringing the conversation to the original topic by saying something along the lines of "It was nice to hear about Rose, tell me more about your fun adventures in Europe though".

Conversation Start - Breaking The Ice

The sound of silence. Sometimes silence is golden. Other times it is awkward. For those that are not naturally blessed with the gift of gab, starting a conversation can be quite a task. The struggle can be evident which can make the person on the other end feel uncomfortable, not to mention the awkward feeling we get.

Once you master the art of small talk, you will never have to worry again. You don't have to dread a dinner party, a first date, or any other potentially awkward event that might put you on the spot, grasping for words to say, and wracking your brain to find something of value to talk about. Talk about nothing! It worked for Seinfeld and it will work for you too.

What is Small Talk?

Small talk is like a snack. It is...just a little piece. It can serve a number of purposes. It might be all you have, just like when you are hiking and you need a protein bar for nourishment. You may have a snack to enjoy while relaxing. A snack can tide you over until a full meal; and it can be a teaser before the main course, similar to an appetizer.

Small talk is when you speak about non-controversial, seemingly unimportant, or trivial matters such as the weather or a sports game you watched on television. Basically, it's talking about nothing. Don't underestimate it, though. "Seinfeld" was a television show about nothing that ran nine straight seasons and was hailed by TV Guide as the World's Best Television Show EVER! Millions tuned in to watch it every week. I know. I was one of them. Almost two decades later, a significant number of people still watch the reruns. I do that too. I actually have many of them memorized. So why do I and so many other people love the show? Personally, I love the fact that I can just enjoy the characters talking about nothing. It requires no concentration, no analysis, no judgements to make or any other kind of thinking. I just get to listen to them talk.

"Hey, Joe! How's the weather?" You might ask your friend. "Fine", he might answer. "You know Texas in July. It's a scorcher but it's not been too bad".

Now, that's small talk. It's a leisure chat about nothing.

When you call your friend in Texas after a tornado and have a talk about the weather, that's quite the contrary. "Hey, Joe! How's the weather?" you might ask. "Oh man", he might reply, "a category 5 touched down right across the street from me. My neighbors are missing and our home is unlivable. We are homeless, Jim. Can we come stay with you for about six months while the insurance fights over our claim?".

Now THAT is...not small talk.

As mentioned before, small talk is a lot like a snack. It can be dished out for different purposes, just as a food snack is. It can tide you over to get to the meat of your conversation. It can serve as the main dish if that suits your purpose. You can small talk for pleasure and you can use small talk to whet your listener's appetite while waiting for the main dish.

Here's How It Is Done

- There are endless approaches to begin your small talk. Here are some of my favorite ways:
- Ask a question. What's even better is to ask a question about the person you are talking to or about something you know interest him.
- Take a look around the room. Something will spark an idea in you. Lay the subject out on the table, providing it isn't about your boss' wife flirting with the Personnel Manager or something inappropriate or controversial. If you see a smart phone and are talking to a tech geek, get his opinion on the latest model that is out.
- Brainstorm. This is done much like the above except, rather than going with what you see, it will be what you think. A bear comes to mind. The person next to you used to live in the mountains of Colorado. Ask if he or she has ever seen a bear there. It's great if you can ease into the small talk by maybe mentioning a bear. "I saw on the news that a camper was attacked by a bear last week. Did you ever encounter one when you lived in Colorado?"
- In the event that the person you are wishing to talk to jumps the gun and asks you a question, feel free to answer with a question. A good way to do so is: "So tell me about your vacation this summer..." You can turn it to focus back on him or her by, "Speaking of vacations, I hear you took a fabulous cruise..." Don't worry. People are

rarely offended by getting to talk about themselves. In fact, you will soon learn that it's quite the contrary.

How to Ask Excellent Questions - Avoid Yes/No Question

Why do people engage in conversations? Usually, it's to obtain understanding about a specific circumstance or to comprehend another person's thoughts. Having the ability to ask appropriate questions is a valuable skill that can positively impact various aspects of your life. While being able to respond to questions indicates intelligence and expertise, being skilled in asking questions demonstrates good decision-making and a desire to learn.

Social Questions – Striking Up Rapport & Moving Beyond Small Talk

Individuals who only discuss their own matters appear to be discourteous and uninteresting. The best way to share the attention in the conversation is by asking questions. A thoughtful inquiry will inspire the other person to talk more and create a connection between the two of you.

If you've ever heard two people talking while they were asking each other meaningful questions, you will know that they can quickly become friends even though they may have just met.

Questions can be used to foster a deeper connection with someone you are already familiar with but have not had a chance to develop a meaningful bond with. Thus, when one has moved past the basic conversation topics, how can one use questioning to get to know the other person better and create conversations that are more engaging?

When I'm helping my clients to ask better questions, I take into account certain principles from psychology. The idea of social reciprocity suggests that when someone does something kind for us, we feel obligated to do something nice in return. This mutual exchange of kindness creates a sense of shared trust and strengthens relationships.

Renowned psychologist Robert Cialdini explains in his book, The Psychology of Persuasion, that individuals who discuss their own experiences and opinions are seen as more favorable than those who concentrate on impersonal or widespread matters. Moreover, when we talk about our life to another person, we usually have more positive feelings for them.

To create an environment of trust and to get your conversation partner to open up, start off by sharing something from your own life or how you're feeling. This will make it easier to ask more personal questions.

If someone shares something intimate with you about themselves or their life, reciprocate by doing the same. Don't ask questions of others if you are not prepared to answer them yourself. Being open and honest in advance will help to make them feel more comfortable. For instance, asking them "What is your biggest dream?" rather than "What is your ultimate dream?" shows that you are willing to be vulnerable and will likely make them feel more trusting of you.

Questions That Build Intimacy: Arthur Aron's Closeness-Generating Procedure

In 1997, Arthur Aron, a psychologist, carried out a study that was a milestone in the social sciences. He joined together people who did not know each other and gave them a list of queries on pieces of paper. Once the couples had completed the questionnaire, they were asked to look into each other's eyes for four minutes. During the study, he discovered that the pairs became more and more close and drawn to one another.

For half of the pairs, they were asked either personal or casual conversation-style questions. People who asked the questions that encouraged closeness experienced a stronger bond and more comfort with their conversation partner.

The lesson to be learned here is that whenever you can, ask questions that go beyond just the facts and figures. For example, Aron's paper provides some examples of the contrast between the two kinds of questions:

Questions for making "small talk":

- What did you do for Halloween last year?
- Where are you from originally?
- Which high school did you attend?
- Questions for creating a closer connection:
- Would you like to be famous? What for?
- What do you consider to be your best achievement?
- What topics should not be joked about?

You should be aware that the questions intended to create closeness need more personal responses and need judgment when deciding when to change from light conversation to significant questions. When you feel a strong connection with the other person, it's okay to gradually shift the conversation to more serious topics. Nevertheless, if the other person looks uncomfortable, be prepared to switch the topic back to something more casual.

Repeat back the last couple of words that someone says in order to motivate them to talk more. This is a simple and unnoticeable way, called the "Parroting" technique, to get more detailed answers.

Repeating a question back to the speaker rather than asking it in full is less formal and I have found it to be a successful technique in almost all cases.

For example:

- You: "Have you ever thought about what it would be like to be famous?"
- Them: "Yes. I'm not sure I would like it. All those photographers..."
- You: "The photographers?"
- Them: "The paparazzi would be chasing after me!"
- You: "Chasing after you?"

Them: "Yes. Did you hear the news about the celebrity who...?"If you pay attention to what someone says, especially if the comments are subtle or not so subtle, you will find they often bring up the same subjects repeatedly. This gives you a great opportunity to ask thoughtful questions that get them talking about what they are most passionate about. I can demonstrate how this works.

At a professional lunch recently, as we sat down, my contact observed some dried mud on her skirt and remarked, "Oh, look at that! That's my pup's doing, he's always leaping up at me when I'm about to go out the door". We then changed the talk to her business and the recent items they had launched.

The woman spoke enthusiastically about their selection of remote webcams and viewing apps, emphasizing how they're great for parents to monitor their kids or babysitters, as well as pet owners. From this, I could tell her real passion was clearly dogs - it's often obvious when someone is really passionate about something, even if the conversation wasn't directly about it.

The meeting was going smoothly, but it didn't quite have the extra enthusiasm that would make it a truly remarkable discussion. During dessert, I mentioned in passing that I was looking forward to seeing my sister soon. I remarked, "It's always nice to be at her farm and get away from the hustle and bustle. And those cute dogs she has! I believe you said you have a dog too...?" After that, I didn't really need to say anything else.

When it was time to say goodbye, she requested that we get together again soon and said I was a great conversationalist, which was only due to me asking a thought-provoking question. This technique can quickly create a bond between people.

Prior to asking a question, seize the moment to shape how the person you are addressing will view it. If you phrase it as "This is an exciting question...", they are more likely to anticipate an engaging query than if you start with "I know this is a basic question, but...".

If you want to create a strong connection with your conversation partner, make sure to phrase your questions in a way that involves both of you, use "we" more often, make sure your question pertains to a meaningful topic. Don't just ask questions that are insignificant or simply seek to pass the time, as these won't help to build a relationship.

In contrast, asking questions such as "Do you think we'll be taken over by the end of the year?" or "Should we all donate more to charity?" will make the other person feel like you are part of the same team and encourage them to share their own views, creating a stronger bond and fostering an engaging conversation.

How To Ask Questions When You Need Factual Answers

Questions with only one purpose in mind—to gather factual information—are commonly used in professional contexts when the focus is on facts rather than opinions. Prior to asking any such question, it's important to be aware of the desired outcome.

Think about your goal when engaging in conversation; whether it's to gain insight into how a department in your company works or to learn the details of a specific procedure. This will help direct the conversation.

Make Sure You're Asking The Right Person

The one who is most knowledgeable about a certain topic isn't always the most suitable to answer your query. We all know people who understand a topic well, but may not be able to share their knowledge effectively. The right person to ask would have a good understanding of the subject, be able to explain it clearly, and have the self-assurance to express their ideas.

It is clear that it may not always be possible to find a person that meets all these requirements, however, these three criteria can assist in narrowing down the choices. This is especially applicable when the query is complex or requires a person with a great deal of expertise.

If you are attempting to get help from someone you are not familiar with to answer an important query, do some preliminary research beforehand. Think about their origin, educational background, hobbies and, if available, their character. Utilizing social media can be a great aid in this instance. If you have a mutual acquaintance, you could ask them for advice. For example, "I'm planning to have a discussion with X on the subject of Y. Do you have any advice on how I can have a successful conversation with them?".

Don't Waste Anyone's Time

Prior to ask someone about something, make sure that you have already tried all of the straightforward solutions. It is very simple to use Google and even if your research does not provide the answers you need, it is still important to demonstrate that you have made an effort.

For example, "I have tried to gain an understanding of the topic by studying the relevant chapter in my textbook and researching online, yet I still find it difficult to comprehend. Would you be able to clarify this for me?".

I have a friend named Jack, he's a computer science professor, who explained me that the students who are least successful are those who lack the creativity to take the initiative. Instead of exploring the numerous online resources to find answers, they tend to send him a message each time they encounter a problem. Even though Jack enjoys imparting his knowledge, these continual inquiries can be quite irksome, at least. He is more likely to be understanding if a student has taken the time to try and figure something out before coming to him for help.

If you feel like someone believes you have taken up too much of their time, inquire about what steps you can take in the future to be more self-sufficient. This gives them the opportunity to direct you to books, websites, and other materials that will enable you to find answers on your own.

When you' think about how to ask your question, it's important to consider the following: begin with the basics if you have any doubts, don't be afraid to ask for a definition of unfamiliar terms. Though it might be a bit awkward, it's better to ask than to make a mistake that could be costly down the road (and take both of you much more time!).

When speaking to someone, it is best to avoid bombarding them with multiple questions at once. Break your inquiries down into a list of individual questions, and put them in a logical order. Consider writing them down before engaging in conversation, even if it may seem a bit ankward with a friend or family member. Taking notes or recording the conversation could also be beneficial if you have a lot of important questions to ask.

Inform the other person in advance if you are about to ask a complicated question so they can prepare to give it their full attention.

Understand when it's appropriate to interject: generally, it's impolite to cut someone off while they are speaking, even if you had just asked them a question. Nevertheless, there are occasions when disrupting is the wisest decision.

Just think about this example: the other person's response to your question is going off topic or doesn't make sense to you, a polite way to re-focus the conversation is to say something like, "I apologize for the interruption, but I just want to make sure I understand...".

If the other person stops talking for a bit or takes a few seconds before responding, don't be anxious; this is actually a sign of respect for your question, it means they're trying to find the best way to answer it, it means they care. Allow them the time they need to think it over. Don't fill the pause by talking yourself, this may disrupt their thinking; let them have the floor.

- Avoid asking questions that try to lead someone to a certain conclusion; instead, if you want to know what someone truly believes, ask them open-ended questions that cannot be answered with a simple yes or no. Some examples:
- Leading question: "What difficulties are you encountering with this project??"
- Non-leading question: "Could you provide me with an update on its progress?"
- Leading question: "Would increased funding for this charity be beneficial?"
- Non-leading question: "What is your opinion of the amount of money we currently give to this charity?"

In the first example, the initial question supposes that the other person is struggling, which would lead them to focus on the unpleasant parts of their experience. The other option, however, provides an opportunity to talk about positive aspects of the situation, leading to a more even-handed evaluation.

In the second example, the suggestive question implies that giving a larger sum of money to the charity is unquestionably beneficial, thereby prompting the listener to concur. On the other hand, the non-suggestive question is unrestrictive, enabling the other party to express their genuine views regarding the amount of the contribution.

If your initial approach fails, consider trying a different one: we all have our unique preferences and habits when it comes to asking and answering questions. For instance, some individuals might not appreciate direct questions and perceive them as aggressive. In case you encounter resistance, don't be discouraged, but think of another way to phrase the question.

Using humor can also be effective in eliciting answers. A lighthearted joke such as "I'm dying of curiosity here!" can ease the tension, help your interlocutor feel at ease, and improve the likelihood of receiving the information you require.

Using Questions To Change Someone's Mind

Questions can serve a dual purpose - not only can they be used to extract information but also to influence and alter someone's perspective. Typically, when people want to persuade others, they present a logical argument or passionately explain why their stance is correct while the other person's viewpoint is wrong. However, this approach often falls short. Once someone senses that you are attempting to change their opinion, they tend to become closed off to your arguments.

Increasing your chances of a good outcome will be helped if you ask the right questions that allow the other person to question their own beliefs. We are more likely to accept an idea if we think it is our own. Thus, by giving the other person the opportunity to think for themselves, you will be more successful than if you try to force your opinion on them

By posing a series of thoughtful questions, someone can be encouraged to examine their perspectives from a different point of view, potentially leading to new revelations. This is a tactic employed by the most successful therapists, as they never dictate what their patients should think. Rather, they use the skill of questioning to help the individual reach their own conclusions. Before a therapist can propose that a patient contemplate the issue from a different perspective, they must be given the chance to vocalize their ideas.

What is someone's opinion on a particular matter? What is their stance on the subject?

- Could you tell me your thoughts on this?
- How do you feel about this subject?
- I'm very curious about your opinion. Would you be willing to share it with me?

Once you have a good grasp of their views, you can motivate them to ponder their convictions by asking the following questions:

- "What led you to reach that conclusion?"
- "When you discuss this topic with others, what are the main counterarguments you hear?"
- "Are there any facts or observations that your theory cannot account for?"
- "What kind of evidence would be needed to persuade you to change your mind on this issue?"
- "Do you have any friends or acquaintances who hold a different perspective on this issue?"

Paying attention to their responses without interrupting will make them feel like their ideas are valued. This will make them more open to considering your own thoughts and examining their own.

Once they are in a receptive mood, it is then appropriate to express your own point of view. It is not certain that they will agree with what you say, but at the least, a respectful dialogue will have taken place.

Asking For A Favor – "Can" Versus "Will"

If you want someone to do you a favor, flattering their ego can help. All you need to do is change "would" or "will" to "can".

"Can you please help me locate the conference center?" is more likely to be answered positively than "Would you please help me find the conference center?" because it prompts the person to consider their own ability to help.

Within themselves, they will come to a conclusion of either "Yes", "No", or "Maybe"; this response is more likely to be based on what they are capable of doing, not whether they would like to help. It is easier to answer "Am I able to do this?" than "Should I help this person?".

It is important to be able to ask the right questions to be successful in a conversation. After having asked a question that was answered in a beneficial way, take a moment to consider how it was asked and remember that technique for future conversations. Keep in mind that the same approach may not work with everyone, and be prepared to adjust your approach accordingly.

How to Stop Fearing Judgment

The most meaningful thing you can perform to get over social anxiety is facing the social events that you are afraid of, rather than avoiding the activities. Avoidance keeps social anxiety going. When you prevent a nerve-wracking event, it may assist you feel okay temporarily; avoidance prevents you from getting very comfortable in social events and understanding how to cope in the long term. The more you keep away from the feared social event, the more worrying it gets.

It prevents you from performing things that you would love to do or achieve particular objectives. For instance, the fear of speaking up may prevent you from sharing your opinions at work.

While it seems not possible to get over a feared social anxiety event, you can overcome it by taking it one step at a time. What is crucial is, to begin with, an event that you can deal with and slowly work your way up to hard situations, developing your coping skills and self-confidence as you move up the anxiety ladder.

To work your way up the social anxiety ladder:

- Do not attempt to face your significant fear instantly. It is not a perfect idea to move quickly or take on too much. This might backfire and enhance your anxiety level.
- Being patient. Getting over social anxiety takes practice and time. It's a slow step by step progress.
- Apply the techniques you have learned to stay calm, for example, concentrating on your challenging negative thoughts and breathing.

Using Empathy in Conversation

What are some ways to convey your willingness to empathize? If you feel that someone is looking to confide in you, you can take certain steps to comprehend their perspective. Refrain from speaking negatively about others and maintain a nonjudgmental tone. The actions and behaviors of other people are often discussed in various conversations, and gossiping occasionally happens to everyone.

If you want someone to trust you, it's important to resist the temptation to gossip or criticize others. People won't feel secure speaking with you if they know you're likely to talk behind their back.

People are hesitant to confide in someone who they believe will be critical of them, as they fear being judged. Therefore, it is important to avoid passing judgment on what your conversation partner is telling you. In addition, it's best to wait for them to ask for advice before offering it.

Demonstrate that you are genuinely interested in what the speaker is saying. Be open, patient, and non-judgmental while they talk and follow the speaker's thought process without interruption. Avoid any signs of rush or frustration and make them feel comfortable and secure when talking to you. Doing so will make them more likely to trust you.

Inquire gently if they have something on their mind. If you notice your conversation partner is tense or distracted, offer them the opportunity to talk by asking if there is anything they would like to discuss. Avoid being forceful and allow them to share if they feel comfortable.

If your conversation partner tells you that something is bothering them but they don't want to discuss it, show empathy by letting them know that you understand and that they can still talk to you about it in the future. Give them the space to fully express themselves. When was the last time you had someone listen to you without interrupting or judging? We all have moments when we just need to share our thoughts and feelings without any constraints.

We can hope that they are understanding of our situation and take the initiative to give us room to express ourselves. If you are the one listening, be sure to let the other person talk until they feel their point has been made. Interrupting can be interpreted as implying that your own ideas are more important than theirs, so try to avoid it.

Carl Rogers, a humanistic therapist, advocated for Unconditional Positive Regard (UPR) when working with clients. He believed that everyone had the capacity to work through their issues, but that they needed the right setting to do so. UPR is a way of creating this supportive environment.

Using the framework proposed by Rogers, you can approach a situation with a nonjudgmental attitude and strive to understand the other person's perspective without letting your own opinions interfere. This doesn't mean that you accept harmful or inappropriate behavior, but rather that you aim to be more understanding and open-minded as you communicate with them.

Assuming the best of another person, that they are good and rational, and that they can grow and change, encourages you to be accepting and understanding.

What To Say When You're Told Something Shocking

Offering someone empathy can be a beautiful thing, but it should come with a warning that the person being offered empathy may be sharing their most inner thoughts, feelings, and experiences, which could be difficult to hear. While some of these secrets may be quite sad, they may also be common experiences that many of us can relate to, such as feeling hopeless after a job loss or feeling deeply depressed after ending a relationship.

Sometimes during a conversation, your partner may reveal something that comes as a shock to you, regardless of how experienced you are or how much you have prepared. It's natural to feel emotional, and it's okay to express those emotions as long as you don't make yourself the center of the conversation.

By expressing empathy through statements like "That sounds terrible to me" or "I feel sad for you," you can make it clear that you care about how they feel while also separating your own emotions from theirs. Remember, it's important to show that you are not a robot and that you understand and empathize with their situation.

Strive to be truthful when responding to their revelations. If they inquire about your emotional reaction, express your genuine feelings. Being sincere and transparent with your emotions can create a sense of safety for the other person to share what is on their mind and heart.

In the event that you have an intense response to what you hear, it is crucial to assure the other person that it is not their fault. Convey to them that you are grateful that they trusted you enough to disclose this information and emphasize that your emotions are your responsibility to handle.

It is important to recognize that not every situation requires a verbal response. It is possible that the person who is sharing their thoughts or feelings with you simply needs someone to listen and empathize, rather than offer advice. In such cases, nonverbal gestures can be just as effective in showing support and understanding.

A gentle touch on their arm, a slow nod of the head, or even a comforting hug (if it is appropriate and welcomed) can convey your empathy and provide comfort. Remember, sometimes just being present and actively listening can be the most powerful response of all.

Improve Communication Skills

The most successful people who eventually go on to become leaders and managers in the workplace are the ones who can make great impressions on everyone they work with because of how well they communicate. Of course, being able to do the job well does play a part of it as well, but when you can meaningfully and effectively communicate with the people you work with, you are already halfway towards success.

At work, we are required to communicate a lot more than we normally would in our everyday lives. We're communicating with clients, with colleagues, with managers, with bosses, through emails, over the phone and even during meetings and presentations. Here is what you can do to improve your communication skills at the workplace:

- Improve Your Body Language – Body language is applicable in the workplace too, perhaps even more so because this is where it really matters. At work, the way you carry yourself and communicate is just as important as how well you get the job done. Remember how our nonverbal cues can speak volumes even when we don't say a word? So, while at work, always adopt confident body language whenever you step into your workplace. Do not slouch, do not fold or cross your arms, do not frown or look sullen. Always be positive, and project a warm and welcoming manner, smile and make eye contact with the people you pass by.
- Avoid Over-Communicating – Avoid being long-winded and beating around the bush when you have discussions and conversations at work. You may think you are trying to be as effective as possible by communicating every little detail, even what is seemingly unnecessary, but avoid doing that because there is such a thing as over-

communicating. Even in presentations, droning on for too long puts you at risk of losing the attention span of your audience. The best way to communicate effectively is to be brief, concise and only communicate what is necessary and relevant to the situation or discussion at hand.

- Seek Feedback – The best way to know if you are effective in what you do, or if what you are doing is working, is to seek feedback honest feedback from your colleagues. Regularly seeking feedback will help you discover what areas you should be working on to improve, and often it is others who can shed better perspective on the things that we may overlook.

- Engage with Your Audience – If you are tasked with presenting at a meeting, this is a great way for you to put into practice your effective communication skills. Now, business presentations are not the most riveting topic, and attention spans will drift eventually, so what do effective communicators do? They engage with their audience. Being effective in your communication requires that you can deliver the points you want to say to an audience that is paying attention. During the meeting or presentation, ask questions and encourage your audience to respond and share their points of view.

- Watching Your Tone of Voice – At the workplace, you need to always ensure that your tone is professional yet friendly and welcoming at the same time. Sometimes it may be necessary to be assertive to stand firm on a point, but still, try and maintain a professional tone when you do that to avoid coming off as aggressive. Effective communication at work requires that you be able to master being confident, direct, professional yet calm and cooperative at the same time.

- Checking Your Grammar – This step is applicable for emails and written communication at the workplace. The most effective communicators are ones who can write flawlessly with no mistakes because they put in the extra effort to check and proofread everything that they type or write before they hit the send button. Check it twice, check it thrice, check it as many times as you need to ensure everything is completely on point before it gets sent. You will impress everyone with your perfect grammar and punctuation, and the ones who read your emails will be able to understand what you are trying to say just as if you were standing there in front of them talking to them.

- Speaking with Clarity – Good communication means being able to be easily understood by everyone you speak to. One of the easiest ways to do that is to simply improve your speech clarity. Pronounce and enunciate your words properly, don't rush through your sentences, don't mumble, don't mutter and avoid using those conversation fillers that were talked about earlier (avoid the um's and ah's): It's important to be clear, concise, and confident when speaking, and avoiding filler words can help achieve this. Practice being able to put forth the messages that you want to say is as few and concise words as possible, this will help you speak with clarity because you already know exactly what needs to be said. Preparing your talking points ahead of time is another great way to boost speech clarity and keep the conversation fillers to a minimum. It also helps avoid excessive and unnecessary talking about irrelevant points, because you want your receiver to be clear about the message, not walk away from the discussion still feeling more confused about it.

- Practice Friendliness – Would you enjoy speaking to someone who is unfriendly and stand-offish at the office? The obvious answer would be no. Nobody would want to engage in a conversation because they would be put off by the person's very demeanor even before they have said a word. To become an effective communicator at work, you need to start adopting a friendly and approachable persona which will encourage your co-workers to want to approach you and have a conversation with you. A friendly approach is even more important when you are having a face-to-face discussion, especially if you are in a managerial position because your colleagues aren't going to want to open up to you if they feel intimidated even before the discussion has properly begun.

- Be Confident – Being confident is an important part of becoming an effective communicator overall. When you interact with others around you at the workplace, the moment you show you are confident you will find it much easier to hold effective conversations with your colleagues and team members that will result in things getting done. Why? Because they are drawn towards your confident approach. Confident people are not thwarted by challenges, they rise to meet them, and this is what people at work want to follow. Somebody who knows what they are doing and is doing it with confidence.

- Say No to Distractions – Meeting rooms exist in the workplace for a reason, and it's time to make full use of them. The best way to have a meaningful conversation with the people you work with is to keep the distractions to a minimum. In an environment like work where so many people are working in close proximity with one another, phones can be constantly ringing off the hook, people will be on the move walking up and down, and several conversations could be going on at once. Not exactly the most conducive environment to hold a discussion, much less an effective conversation. Keep the distractions to a minimum, go into a meeting room and close the door, put the phones away and then when both parties are ready, begin your conversation.

- Keep Your Points Consistent – To be able to deliver messages effectively means you need to be able to remain on point and consistent with what you are saying. It helps if you stick to the facts and the focus of the discussion at hand, write down and prepare your talking points before you hold the conversation. Your points should flow smoothly, and nothing should contradict each other because you could end up confusing the receiver of your message and they become unsure about what it is you are trying to say. Your key points of your message are also at risk of being lost when you contradict yourself far too much. Plan and prepare ahead, make some notes and have them ready if you need to refer to them to help you stay on course. This is how you practice becoming a more effective communicator.

- Remain as Transparent as Possible – There is nothing that is disliked more at the workplace than a lack of transparency. If you are in a leadership position especially, transparency is important in your efforts to become a more effective communicator overall. Never try to hide information, or leave out bits and pieces of information when working with your colleagues on a project or working in a team. It makes it difficult for everyone involved to communicate well if they don't have all the necessary information on hand to work with. If you are the one that is in charge of a team project, communicate clearly with your peers on what the deadlines and the goals of the project are, and ensure that everyone is clear on what needs to be done before moving forward.

Persuasive Communication

By definition, persuasion is the act of making an effort to convince someone to do something or change their beliefs in favor of some that you think are worthwhile. Empathy cannot lead you to persuasion because it causes you to see that the other person is right in his own right. However, if you fully understand where a person is coming from, you can strategize and come up with a way to persuade him or her to change his or her mind. This is why persuasion is said to be an art.

You see, art is any activity that a person uses to express the emotions buried inside. It conveys complex messages that words wouldn't carry. It, however, can be intellectually challenging, complex, and coherent. That said, the product of your art must be an original piece. It, therefore, demands a great deal of skill and patience.

The art of persuasion does not check all boxes in the definition of art because people take various approaches to persuasion. Some will persuade without even showing an ounce of emotion while others are all about the emotional appeal. In addition, you cannot talk of persuasion as an art in the sense that other art forms like music and paintings are. It is also easy to persuade without intending to be unique in any way. However, persuasion does indeed contain other qualities that qualify it to be an art: it is complex, intellectually challenging, it conveys a complex message, it can be quite original, and it highlights your point of view.

You may wonder what the point of persuading is. Why should you waste your precious time and energy persuading others? Isn't it also a form of manipulation? The truth is that you need to learn how to persuade others to achieve any success in life. Every seller has had to persuade a customer to buy his or her products. Every teacher has had to persuade parents that he can do a good job. Every married person has had to persuade his or her partner to marry him or her. Every employee has had to persuade the employer to hire him. Every successful politician has had to persuade voters to vote for him.

As you can see, almost every success in life demands that you convince others that you have the capacity to fit and fulfill the mandates of the position you intend to fill. Persuasion seems to run in the bedrock of every human endeavor.

The Basics of Persuasion

The following are the principles of persuasion. govern the ability to convince people to share your ideologies and points of view:

Scarcity

People are more drawn to people, products, or opportunities that are exclusive or limited in edition. When people perceive an impending shortage, they tend to demand scarce resources, and if they can be bought, they buy them in excess.

Companies take advantage of this tendency and suggest shortages in their supply (only five pieces remaining), limiting the time an offer is available (available for three days only), or suggesting scarcity in the frequency with which an offer is made (annual sale). Customers, driven by

63

the fear of missing out, respond by making purchases, most of which are unplanned and impulsive.

In life, everything is measured by its relative value. If someone thinks something is valuable, I will be driven to accord the same value to the item. We often want to own things because others have them. As such, if you want something to be considered valuable, you must make it scarce, and that includes yourself too. In communication, if you want people to value your words, talk less.

Reciprocity

Whenever you do good to someone, there is a natural nagging and drive to reciprocate the gesture. This behavior is ingrained in human DNA so that we can help each other survive. Interestingly, you also could tip the reciprocity scale to favor you disproportionately by giving some small gestures that show your consideration to others, and when you ask for some help or a favor, the others will happily offer it.

Authority

It is impossible to persuade anyone to do something when you do not appear to have expertise or knowledge in that field. No one wants to be led to the shaky ground of trial and error. A persuader must radiate special skills and expertise. Experts are more likely to be trusted. They radiate authority in their fields. Therefore, when you intend to persuade a person to take a particular stand, ensure that your knowledge and familiarity with that subject or field is beyond reproach. When you do this, you will build your reputation as an expert or personality in that particular field.

Liking

One of the impossible tasks is to convince an enemy to do anything. It is an exercise in futility. No one trusts or likes dealing with someone they consider unpleasant. What if you are dealing with strangers, how do you get them to like you? It's very simple. You only need to appear open, kind, attentive, sympathetic, and empathetic. Also, let people know that they are highly regarded and appreciated. Appreciation is demonstrated through acts such as giving presents, inviting the people to special events, offering 'inside' information, and by making regular phone calls. People also appreciate feeling that you understand them and their interests. If you have the chance, give valuable ideas or suggestions, and you will have them eating from the palm of your hand.

Consistency and Commitment

Consistency assures a person that he or she will get the results he or she expects or got in a previous similar engagement. Before people commit themselves to you, they want to see signs that you are committed too, and consistent in your giving results. The best thing is to give these signs of commitment and consistency step by step, and the other party will slowly buy into your ideas.

For example, when dealing with a customer that wants to buy a dress, create the consistency that convinces the customer that you are best suited to sell the dress. You could say, "Yes, we have the dress in red, yes we have a changing room where you can try on your dress, yes, we can also deliver the dress to you, yes, we have an in-house seamstress who will make your preferred alterations for free, yes, you can carry your dress home today." Ensure that all the customer's concerns can be addressed, and when you

65

are done, the customer will have no choice but to stick with you.

Suppose a friend or coworker calls asking if he or she can come over to share some personal information, show that you are committed to listening to what the friend has to say, and to doing all you can to help. Say, "Yes, I am available to speak to you now (or in a little while), I promise that our conversation will be confidential, you are free to speak to me about anything, I will help you as much as I can, you have my complete attention." When you say this, the individual will likely feel safe and will want to speak about the issue of concern. After the conversation, assure the individual that you will be available to talk when called upon to do so.

Social Proof and Consensus

People are the ultimate advertising tools; when someone thinks of you or the items you are selling to be good, be sure that he or she will make that known to other people the person comes into contact with. What's more, human beings tend to be more convincing than other ad methods. For example, a customer is more likely to read customer reviews and to believe them, over and above ads on various media platforms. Therefore, as you market yourself and your products or services, always refer to those who would have something positive to say, such as references in your resume or happy customer reviews. Their opinions will be more convincing than anything you would say to market yourself.

How to Persuade Someone of Your Opinion

Having understood what persuasion is and the principles that govern it, let's now see how to go about it. The first thing you ought to keep in mind is that you can persuade anyone, naturally, without even trying much. The following steps and techniques will teach you how to influence, from a marketing and a personal perspective, but these techniques are viable in any interpersonal engagement you are involved in, from making new friends, convincing an employer to hire you, networking, and relating with friends. They include:

Take Up Mirroring To Help Create A Subconscious Agreement With The Other Party

Mirroring is presumed to be one of the easiest and quickest ways to create accord between two parties. It refers to the acts of copying someone's volume, speed of speech, tone and body language in a bid to reflect that person's behavior to him or her, just like a mirror would reflect.

Research shows that mirroring a person's behavior produces more considerable social influence over the person being mimicked. The study found that individuals who mirrored had more success persuading the other party, and were regarded with more positivity than those who did not mirror.

The reason mirroring works so well is because behaving like the other person is behaving tends to put the individual at ease, which increases the possibilities of building a rapport with them. It breaks through any form of subconscious resistance the person may have and encourages the individual to trust you.

Typically, people mirror others subconsciously, but when you are learning how to do it for persuasion, you must do it consciously, until when it comes to you on autopilot so that it now is a natural part of your interactions. The easiest way to start is to try to match the other party's conversation tempo and stance. However, you do not just jump into it immediately. One cardinal rule of thumb is to wait it out, about 5 to 10 seconds before you start mirroring the other party's stance so that your attempts are not too noticeable.

Remember that your mission here is to gain trust, not to arouse suspicion.

Be careful that mirroring sometimes backfires, especially when you mirror negativity such as raising your voice when another raises his or taking up negative postures like crossing your legs or your arms. Turning your body away from the individual also communicates negativity. Be careful not to do any of them.

Be Surrounded by Other Influential Persons

The law of averages states that the result of any particular situation is the average of all possible outcomes. Jim Rohn brought a new perspective to this law saying that a person is the average of five people he or she hands out with most of the time. He said this in reference to the fact that while we interact with hundreds or thousands of people in daily life, only a few of those have an impact on us. Their influence is very significant, to the point that they influence how we speak, how we think, how we talk, and how we react to situations, among others.

Whenever you keep the company of people you aspire to be like, you will naturally begin to emulate them, and will eventually have risen to their level. Therefore, when you want to learn how to persuade and influence other people, you have to keep the company of some influential people so that you be in a position to absorb their mannerisms, reasoning, general outlook on life and their knowledge because these are the factors that have contributed towards their success.

We all have the privilege of choosing our friends, the people we spend our time with, and it is better that you select people that are going to make you a better person, and make it easier for you to reach the goals you intend to achieve in life, one of which is to become an influential person.

Encourage the Other Party To Talk About Himself

People like speaking their minds. Science confirms that about 30 t0 40 percent of the words we speak are solely about ourselves. We love expressing our viewpoints, talking about our experiences, achievements, and others. Some are even comfortable talking about the struggles they are going through because it gives them some form of relief and eases the stress in their minds. When scientists studied the brain as people spoke about themselves, and scans showed some activity in parts of the brain that are primarily linked to value and motivation. It is this same brain area that is linked with a person talking about himself, and other thrills such as drug use, sex, and money.

Start with some small talk, then proceed with some meaningful questions. As the person speaks, keenly listen to the answer given, and where possible turn the answer around into a follow-up question to let the speaker know that you are enjoying their talk. This encouragement causes the other party to go deeper and reveal information he or she did not intend to give.

As the individual continues speaking, you will have a broader look into who they are, what they believe, and you will also figure out the areas of common ground so that it becomes easier to make a personal connection with them. The more you listen, the higher chance you stand to influence the person.

Take Advantage of the Pauses and Moments of Silence

As we mentioned before, silence is uncomfortable for many people. It makes them feel prompted to speak to fill it. An influential person must be fully aware of the effect that silence has on people, and use it to his or her advantage. Use silence to make the other party disclose some more information, give clues, or even make a mistake that could be to your advantage.

On the other hand, when you indicate that you are not afraid of silence so that you are unhurried and more deliberate in your speech and your actions, you elicit a feeling of confidence and control. Therefore, even in uncomfortable situations, be patient in your discourse, and you will appear confident.

Another advantage of the silence and the pauses is that they allow you to process the information you get better. You also get the time to consider the best approach for communicating some thoughts, so that you present your ideas in a humane, empathetic way that will help deepen the connection you have with others.

How to Improve Persuasive Communication

Sometimes persuasive communication does not work because:

- The person receiving the information does not trust the communicator
- They believe there is some hidden truth
- There is conflicting information about a particular situation
- If the information is not helpful

In order to improve your persuasive communication skills:

Know Your Audience

When using persuasive communication, it is important to understand your audience or the individual person you are communicating with. Persuasive communication becomes effective if it addresses the audience's needs or if the audience feels that, they can relate to the communicator in some way. One of the challenges here is because the audience has the power of choice, and the communicator is trying to influence them to make a particular choice.

Capture Their Attention

To capture the audience's attention, you need to be credible, influential, and authoritative. People pay close attention to authoritative figures or industrial leaders because they feel that they have something they can share with them and therefore have to be keen on what they are saying. This is why a good number of companies use celebrities to market their brands. Another way to capture the audience's attention is to use facts and figures, people are more inclined to listen when you have proof in comparison to just telling them to believe you.

Use Of Body Language

When communicating verbally, body language influences your ability to persuade as much as your words. When you fidget a lot, it comes out as if you are not certain of the information you are trying to covey or when you cross your arms, you come out as aggressive or hostile. Avoiding eye contact also shows that you are hiding something. In order to be more persuasive, you need to relax, avoid crossing your arms, use gestures and always maintain eye contact.

Tailor Your Message

Ideally, people have a chance of persuading other people more when communicating with them face-to-face. One of the advantages of this is that if an audience has follow-up questions, they can get immediate responses. In order to improve persuasive communication, it is important to tailor the message to the audience. You cannot use jargon when communicating with kids, instead, use simple language.

Communicate Their Benefits

In order to improve your persuasive communication skills, you need to convince your audience how what you are proposing will benefit them. If you are trying to get people to buy a particular brand, tell them the benefits they get over other brands.

Ensure Your Message Is Understood

When persuading either an audience or individual, it is important to ensure they understand your message before you get to the persuading part. Clarify or rephrase what you are trying to say for other people to understand it before you can persuade them.

Do It Repetitively

Another way to improve your persuasive skills is to do it repetitively. People rarely get on-board the first time around but when they hear it again and again even from other people, they get interested. This is the reason ads on media play several times a day. However, be careful not to oversell.

Be Honest and Truthful

It is important for the audience to build trust with the persuader before they can be persuaded. Always ensure that whatever you are selling truly does what you say. Sell something legit.

Everyone uses persuasive communication in his or her day-to-day life, therefore following the tips outlined above will enable you to hone up on your persuasive skills.

The Definition of a Rapport and the Process of Creating It

Rapport is the process of developing a connection with someone else. It forms the basis for meaningful and harmonious relationships between people. People can build rapport either instantly or over time. You develop a rapport with someone when:

- You both have positive thoughts and feelings about each other
- You are both friendly and show care and concern
- You both share a common understanding

A number of things like body language, eye contact and tempo can be beneficial in building rapport.

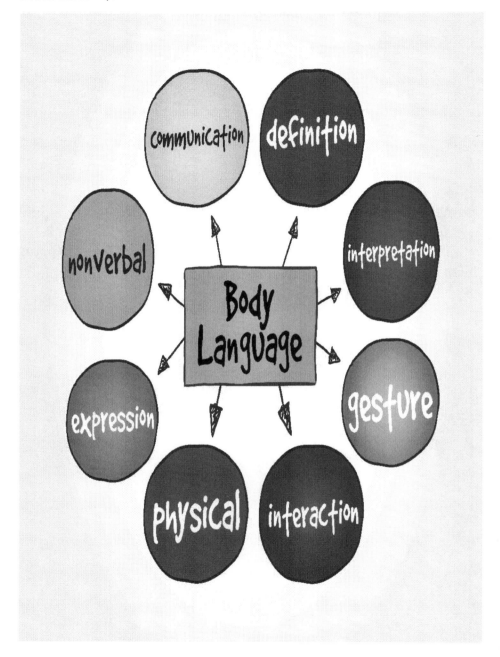

Body Language

Body Language in Communication

Non-verbal form of contact is a tremendously difficult yet vital part of general communication abilities. Conversely, individuals are frequently unconscious of their non-verbal actions. Researchers connect big significance to the individuals' ability for verbal communication. However, people have a corresponding path of nonverbal contact, which might disclose more than our cautiously selected language. Most of the nonverbal gestures and understanding of pointers is involuntary and carried out beyond our awareness and power. On the other hand, using our nonverbal signals we unsuspectingly convey plenty of messages regarding our physical and mental states. The signs we bring out, the pose in which we embrace our hands, the expressions we put on our bodies and the nonverbal persona of our talking contribute to how other people perceive us.

A fundamental responsiveness of nonverbal contact approaches, above what is stated might assist in developing communication with other people. The familiarity of these secret languages might be employed to support individuals to speak about their worry and may result in a superior understanding, which is the function of interaction. When we speak regarding body language, we consider the delicate signals we give and get to from others nonverbally. Several individuals wish to understand how to interpret body language. Body language might be clustered into a few categories:

Facial expressions

Scholars revealed seven widespread micro-expressions or small facial signals every person portrays if they feel a powerful feeling. People are attracted to observing the face to know if somebody has concealed feelings. The small signals shown on our faces are a vital element of nonverbal communication.

Body Proxemics

This is an expression that refers to the study of how we use physical space and distance in communication. We are continuously observing how somebody is moving, making gestures, leaning, shifting forward or backwards. Body activities notify people a lot regarding inclination and anxiety. Movements are involved in body language signals.

Ornaments

Outfit, necklaces, hairstyles, are all added to the nonverbal indicators. Not only do specific paints and fashions send indicators to other people, how we interrelate with our ornaments is as well important. Is somebody an adorer of his or her phone? Do they continuously touch their necklace? We must notice these vital body language signals.

Interpretation of body language

Reading body language might sound like a difficult task; however, mastering the art of interpreting them is vital. There are two methods of understanding body language in other people. Decoding is the capability of reading people's prompts. It entails how people read concealed feelings, information, and traits from an individual nonverbal signal. Encoding is the skill of sending signals to other persons. Encoding plays a key role in controlling your individual trademark. The first feeling you provide and the way you make someone think when you meet them for the first time.

Significance of nonverbal cues in interactions

Emphasizing what is stated verbally.

For instance, individuals might nod energetically when meaning yes to emphasize that they concur with the other individual. A gesticulation of the shoulders and a gloomy face when stating, "I am okay, thank you" might mean that matters are not all right at all.

Convey information about their emotional state.

Someone's facial appearance, his or her pitch of tone, and his or her body language might notify somebody precisely what you are undergoing, even when he or she has barely uttered a sentence.

Strengthen the link between persons

When you have observed partners discussing, you might have detected that they have a tendency of mirroring one another's nonverbal signals. They place their arms in parallel poses, they laugh uniformly, and they look at each other frequently. These activities strengthen their affair; consequently, building on their relationship, and assist them to feel coupled.

Offer response to the other individual.

Laughing and nodding inform somebody that you are paying attention and that you concur with what they are putting across. Body shifting and hand signs might point out that you desire to talk. These slight signs provide information quietly but unmistakably.

Normalize the course of interaction

There are several signs that people use to inform others that he or she has completed or wish to talk. A resounding nod and strong closure of the lips show that someone has no intention of speaking anymore. Maintaining eye contact with the person in charge of a conference and nodding faintly shall show that you desire to talk.

Features of Body Language

There are types of body language. This is because we cannot classify the different styles in the same category. Different body languages can be distinguished. So, which body language styles can be differentiated? Generally, the body language is divided into two columns. That includes; Body parts and the Intent

So what kinds in each class can be observed?

Let us start with the body parts and the language they communicate.

- The Head - The placement of the head and its movement, back and forth, right to left, side to side, including the shake of hair.
- Face - This includes facial expressions. You should note that the face has many muscles ranging from 54 and 98 whose work is to move different areas of the face. The movements of the face depict the state of your mind.
- Eyebrows - The eyebrows can express themselves through moving up and down, as well as giving a frown
- Eyes - The eyes can be rolled, move up down, right, and left, blink as well as the dilatation
- The Nose - The expression of the nose can be by the flaring of the nostrils and the formation of wrinkles at the top

- The Lips - There are many roles played by the lips, that include snarling, smiling, kissing, opened, closed, tight, and puckering
- The Tongue - The tongue can roll in and out, go up and down, touch while kissing, and also the licking of lips
- The Jaw - The jaw opens and closes, it can be clinched and also the lower jaw can be moved right and left
- Your Body Posture - This describes the way you place your body, legs, and arms connected, and also concerning other people
- The Body Proximity - This looks at how far your body is to other people
- Shoulder Movements - They move up and down, get hunched, and hang
- The Arm - These go up down, straight and crossed

Legs and the feet-these can have an expression in many different ways. They can be straight, crossed, legs placed one over the other, the feet can face the next person you are in a conversation with, they can face away from each other, the feet can be dangling the shoes

The hand and the fingers-the way that your hands and fingers move is powerful in reading other people's gestures. The hands can move up and down, they can do some hidden language that only people of the same group can understand.

How one reacts to handling and placing of objects-this is not regarded as a body part but it technically plays a role in reading a body language. This may predict anger, happiness and much more.

This includes willingly making body movements otherwise known as gestures. These are the movements that you intended to make for example shaking of hands, blinking your eyes, moving, and shaking your body in a sexy way maybe to lure someone and much more. There are also involuntary movements-this are movements that you have no control over. This can be sweating, laughter, crying and much more. Facial Expression

The face, which includes the eyes, is a crucial tool for conveying emotions and attitudes. By becoming familiar with and observing facial expressions in action (rather than just as a fixed feature), we can gain deeper insight into the messages that others are trying to convey to us.

Based on our observations, we tend to make assumptions about people's personalities and other characteristics from their facial features. For instance, people with good looks are usually ascribed certain qualities regardless of whether or not they really have them.

The face and first impressions

During the initial encounter between two individuals, the initial five minutes are of utmost importance. Perceptions that are created in this brief period generally stay with them for a long time, and even after that, any behavior will be judged through the lens of those initial views.

The face is a very important factor in helping to create relationships with other people. In a short span of time, we can form judgments about someone's character, their intelligence, and even their suitability as a friend or partner. These conclusions can be based mainly on facial features.

Talking to the face

Our face and eyes are our best way to communicate without speaking. We rely on it to show how kind we are, our emotions, and how much we pay attention to others. Facial expressions can be used to emphasize words, such as when a mother reprimands her child: the expression on her face will show if she's truly mad or just a bit annoyed.

The face is the primary way to express emotions through body language, but other body parts can also be used to communicate. Therefore, it's important to consider more than just the face when trying to interpret a message.

There is a wide variety of facial expressions, but Paul Ekman and Wallace Friesen have identified six primary emotions that most of us can recognize reliably.

The smiles

Smiles can come in a variety of sizes and intensity, from a slight upturn of the lips to a wide grin. They are often used as a friendly sign of greeting, to display a range of positive emotions such as joy, pleasure, and happiness. Even those who are born without vision are known to smile when something pleases them. Smiles are often seen as attractive and joyous, though they can also be used to conceal other feelings.

• Hide the struggles behind a smile.

• Offer a smile as a response of acceptance.

• Smile to make trying times easier.

• Smile to draw in the grins of others.

• Smile to ease the strain.

• Smile to conceal anxiety.

• Grief, discontentment and gloom

These emotions are characterized by a lack of expression, a downward turn of the mouth, a lowered gaze, and a general drooping of the facial features. Speech is often quiet and slow. While they may be hard to distinguish from one another, there are other physical indicators that can help identify the emotion being expressed.

• Sadness

• Eyebrows slightly angled towards the ears forming a semi-circle.

• Shoulders slouching.

• Corners of the mouth at 45% of their usual height.

• Hands clasped together and facing downwards.

• Disappointment

• Eyebrows not fully raised.

• Glancing backwards, usually to the left, and downwards.

• Shoulders slightly slouched and hands by the sides of the body.

• Depression

• Eyebrows normally raised.

• Corners of the mouth slightly descending.

• Shoulders completely slumped.

• Legs and thighs parallel.

• Hands together and facing downwards.

It's important to remember that everyone experiences emotions differently; no two people will show their emotions in the same way.

Dislike / contempt

The facial expression associated with this reaction is one that only affects the central area of the face. It is characterized by narrowing of the eyes, pursing of the lips, a wrinkling of the nose and a turning away of the head from the source of the reaction. The upper lip is raised on one end while the other remains in its normal position.

Anger

When someone is angry, it is often shown through a piercing gaze, a tight-lipped expression, and a furrowed brow. Their hands may be clenched together as if to contain the emotion.

The fear

Fear can manifest in various physical expressions that are not limited to a single form. These expressions can include widened eyes, an open mouth, or a general tremor that affects both the face and the rest of the body.

The interest

When it comes to nonverbal communication, one of the most noticeable signs is often the "bird head," where someone tilts their head at a certain angle to show interest. Other aspects to pay attention to are their eyes, which may be more open than normal, or their mouth slightly open. It's important to also be aware of the influence that body language complements have on the perception of others – they can be a factor in whether or not the intended message is conveyed successfully. By being mindful of these nuances of nonverbal communication, we can better utilize it to our advantage.

Other information about the face

Facial expressions can be used to reveal emotions, showcase one's personality, indicate interest in another person, and show how much they are engaging in conversation. They can be used to express feelings, attitudes, and even sexual attraction and allure.

Studies have indicated that there are variations between genders when it comes to the use of facial expressions for communication. Females tend to smile and chuckle more frequently than males, which may not always be due to them enjoying the moment but instead being a bit uncomfortable. On the other hand, men may appear more stern, but this is not necessarily a sign of displeasure or lack of engagement.

Facial expression is constantly shifting while conversing. These brief "micro" expressions, lasting only a fraction of a second, are a good indication of how someone truly feels.

Posture

Expectedly, posture and body orientation should be interpreted in the context of the entire body language to develop the full meaning being communicated.Starting with an open posture, it is used to denote friendliness.

One can appear more persuasive by standing or sitting upright with their feet spread apart and their hands facing outward. This is known as open posture. To attain this position, one should stand or sit upright with the head held high, chest and stomach exposed. Combining this open stance with a tranquil facial expression and proper eye contact creates an inviting and composed demeanor. Keep the body oriented towards the other person during conversation.

A closed posture can also be seen where one crosses their arms across their chest, crosses their legs away from others, sits in a hunched forward position and shows the backs of their hands and clenches their fists. This stance gives the impression that the individual is bored, hostile or detached, and is displaying caution and a readiness to defend themselves against any accusation or threat.

Having a confident posture can demonstrate to others that you are not anxious, nervous, or stressed. To obtain such a posture, one should stand tall and keep their head held high with their eyes level. The shoulders should be pulled back, and arms and legs should be relaxed. This type of posture is often used in formal settings such as while giving a presentation, while being cross-examined, or during a project presentation.

Equally important there is postural echoing and is used as a flirting technique by attracting someone in the guardian. It is attained by observing and mimicking the style of the person and the pace of movement. When the individual leans against the wall, replicate the same. By adjusting your postures against the others to attain a match you are communicating that you are trying to flirt with the individual. The postural echoing can also be used as a prank game to someone you are familiar with and often engage in casual talk.

Maintaining a straight posture communicates confidence and formality. Part of the confidence of this posture is that it maximizes blood flow and exerts less pressure on the muscle and joints which enhances the composure of an individual. The straight posture helps evoke desirable mood and emotion which makes an individual feel energized and alert. A straight posture is highly preferred informal conversations such as during meetings, presentation or when giving a speech.

Having a slumped posture and curved back is seen as a sign of disinterest and can give off the impression of being sluggish, sorrowful, or poverty-stricken. A slumped position implies a strain to the body which makes the individual feel less alert and casual about the ongoing conversation. On the other hand, leaning forward and maintaining eye contact suggests that one is listening keenly. During a speech, if the audience leans forward in an upright position then it indicates that they are eager and receptive to the message.

Furthermore, if one slants one of the shoulders when participating in a conversation then it suggests that the individual is tired or unwell. Leaning on one side acutely while standing or sitting indicates that you are feeling exhausted or fed up with the conversation and are eagerly waiting for the end or for a break. Think of how you or others reacted when a class dragged on to almost break time. There is a high likelihood that the audience slanted one of their shoulders to the left or right direction. In this state, the mind of the individual deviates from things that one will do next. In case of a tea break, the mind of the students will deviate from what one will do during or after the tea break.

By the same measure standing on one foot indicates that one is feeling unease or tired. When one stands on one foot then it suggests that the person is trying to cope with uncomforting. The source of uneasiness could be emotional or physiological. For instance, you probably juggled your body from one foot to help ease the need to go for a short call or pass wind. In most cases, one finds himself or herself standing on one foot when an uncomfortable issue is mentioned. It is a way to disrupt the sustained concentration that may enhance the disturbing feeling.

If one cups their head or face with their hands and rests the head on the thighs then the individual is feeling ashamed or exhausted. When the speaker mentions something that makes you feel embarrassed then one is likely to cup their face or head and rest the face on the thighs. It is a literal way of hiding from shame. Children are likely to manifest this posture though while standing. When standing this posture may make one look like he or she is praying.

Additionally, if one holds their arms akimbo while standing then the individual is showing a negative attitude or disapproval of the message. The stance is made by clasping the waist with both hands while standing tall and facing the person you are addressing. The hands should simultaneously grip on the flanks, the part near the kidneys. In most cases, the arms-akimbo posture is accompanied by disapproval or sarcastic face to denote attitude, disdain or disapproval.

When one stretches both of their shoulders and arms and rests them on chairs on either side then the individual is feeling tired and casual. The posture is akin to a static flap of wings where one stretches their shoulder and arms like wings and rests them on chairs on either side. It is one of the postures that loudly communicates that you are bored, feeling casual and that you are not about the consequences of your action. The posture is also invasive of the privacy and space of other individuals and may disrupt their concentration.

If one bends while touching both of their knees, then the individual is feeling exhausted and less formal with the audience. The posture may also indicate extreme exhaustion and need to rest. For instance, most soccer players bend without kneeling while holding both of their knees, indicating exhaustion. Since in this posture one is facing down, the posture may be highly inappropriate in formal contexts and may make one appear queer.

When one leans their head and supports it with an open palm on the cheeks then it indicates that one is thinking deep and probably feeling sad, sorrowful or depressed. The posture is also used when one is watching something with a high probability of negative outcomes such as a movie or a game. The posture helps one focus deep on the issue akin to meditating.

Additionally, crossing your arms to touch shoulders or touch the biceps indicates that one is deliberately trying to focus on the issue being discussed. Through this posture, an individual will try to avoid distractions and think deeper about what is being presented. If you watch European soccer you will realize that coaches use this posture when trying to study the match, especially where their team is down. However, this posture should not be used in formal contexts as it suggests rudeness. The posture should be used among peers only.

Then there is the crossing of the legs from the thigh through the knee while seated on a chair especially on a reclining chair. In this posture, one is communicating that he or she is feeling relaxed and less formal.

Generally, this type of stance is seen when someone is viewing a movie in the comfort of their own home or when they are still in the office after their shift has ended. If this posture is replicated in a formal context then it suggests boredom or lack of concentration.

When sitting with crossed legs, it can be interpreted as a sign that someone is attempting to concentrate in a relaxed setting like at home. For instance, if a wife or a child asks the father about something that he has to think through then the individual is likely to exhibit this posture. If this posture is replicated in a formal context then it suggests boredom or lack of concentration.

Eye Contact

Reading eye contact is important to understand the true status of an individual, even where verbal communication seeks to hide it. As advised, body language should be read as a group, we will focus on individual aspects of body language and make the reader understand how to read that particular type of body language.

Your pupils dilate when you are focused and interested in someone you are having a conversation with, or the object we are looking at or using. The pupils will contract when one is transiting from one topic to another. We have no control over the working of pupils. When one is speaking about a less interesting topic, the pupils will contract.

Effective eye contact is critical when communicating with a person. Eye contact implies that one looks but does not stare. Persistent eye contact will make the recipient feel intimidated or judged. In Western cultures, regular eye contact is desired, but it should not be overly persistent. If one offers constant eye contact, then it is seen as an attempt to intimidate or judge, which makes the recipient of the eye contact uncomfortable. There are studies that suggest that most children fall victim to attacks by pet dogs if they make too much eye contact, as this causes them to feel threatened and react defensively and instinctually.

Winking

In Western culture, winking is considered as a form of flirting which should be done to people we are in good terms with.

This varies, though, as Asian cultures frown on winking as a facial expression.

Blinking

In most cases, blinking is instinctive; our affection for the person we are speaking to causes us to subconsciously blink faster. If the average rate of blinking is 6 to 10 times per minute, then it can indicate that one is drawn to the person they are speaking to.

Eye Direction

The direction of the eyes tells us about how an individual is feeling. When someone is thinking, they tend to look to their left as they are recalling or reminiscing. An individual that is thinking tends to look to their right when thinking creatively, but it can also be interpreted as a sign that one is lying. For left-handed people, the eye directions will be reversed.

Avoiding Eye Contact

When we do not make eye contact with someone we are speaking to for extended periods of time, we are most likely uncomfortable with the person or the conversation. We avoid looking someone in the eye if we feel ashamed to be communicating at them. When we feel dishonest about trying to deceive people, we avoid looking at them. While it is okay to blink or drop eye contact temporarily, people that consistently shun making eye contact are likely to be feeling uneasy with the message or the person they are communicating with. For emphasis, staring at someone will make them drop eye contact due to feeling intimidated. Evasive eye contact happens where one deliberately avoids making eye contact.

Crying

Human beings cry due to feeling uncontrollable pain or in an attempt to attract sympathy from others. Crying is considered an intense emotion associated with grief or sadness though it can also denote extreme happiness known as tears of joy. When an individual forces tears to manipulate a situation, this is referred to as "crocodile tears." Typically, though, if one cries, then the individual is likely experiencing intense negative emotion.

Additionally, when one is interested in what you are speaking, he or she will make eye contact often. This is not entirely eye contact, though. Rather, the eye contact on the eyes of the other person is for the duration of 2-3 minutes, and then it switches to the lips or nose, and then returns to the eyes. For a brief moment, the person initiating eye contact will look down then back up to the eyes. Looking up and to the right demonstrates dismissal and boredom. Dilation of the pupil may indicate that someone is interested or that the room is brighter.

In some instances, sustained eye contact may be a signal that you want to speak to the person or that you are interested in the person sexually. At one point, you have noticed a hard stare from a man towards a particular woman to the point the woman notices and asks the man what is all that for. In this case, eye contact is not being used to intimidate but to single out the target person. You probably have seen a woman ask why is that man staring at me then she proceeds to mind her business but on taking another look at the direction of the man the stare is still there. In this manner, eye contact is used to single out an individual and make them aware that one is having sexual feelings towards the person.

However, people are aware of the impact of body language and will seek to portray the expected body language. For instance, an individual that is lying is likely to make deliberate eye contact frequently to sound believable. At one point, you knew you were lying but went ahead to make eye contact. You probably have watched movies where one of the spouses is lying but makes believable eye contact with others. The reason for this faked body language is because the person is aware of the link between making eye contact and speaking the truth.

Like verbal language, body language and in particular eye contact can be highly contextual. For instance, an individual may wink to indicate that he or she agrees with the quality of the product being presented or that he or she agrees with the plan. Eye contact in these settings can be used as a coded language for a group of people. At one point, one of your classmates may have used a wink to indicate that the teacher is coming or to indicate that the secret you have been guarding is now out.

Gestures

Hand gestures, in general, are rather accidental. They are important in telling us a lot about another person who utilizes his or her hands when talking, though. Also, in the case of arm movement, there are guidelines for constructive body language.

Leave Your Arms in An Open Position

The first step is to always have an outstretched hand. Open hands imply transparency and approval. Open palms mean honesty and integrity as well. There's also a way to read the open palms, though. If the hands are open when speaking or facing down, this means the individual's attitude is somewhat dominant. This is particularly noticeable in the case of handshakes. Nevertheless, it is a non-threatening indication if the palms are opened and facing upwards. This individual is accessible and can be perceived in essence as welcoming. The palms switch, therefore, totally alters the manner we are viewed by others.

Don't Cross the Arms

While talking, the arms ought not to be crossed and the hands must not be caught. Fastened hands show the absence of responsibility and the absence of certainty. Crossed arms show guarded or anxious position. It has likewise been seen that on when an individual stand with his arms crossed, at that point he gets little on of the discussion when contrasted with an individual with great affection with open arms. Additionally, protective non-verbal communication likewise prompts lower maintenance control.

It is in our normal nature to fold our arms to feel great. Be that as it may, thinks about have demonstrated that such a non-verbal communication is seen as adverse by individuals. Besides, held clench hands are additionally a major no during discussions. The arms ought not to go underneath the midsection level and should consistently be raised over the abdomen while talking. The arms can at times go down however it ought not to be so all through the discussion.

Do Not Grip Your Arms

While addressing somebody, don't grasp your arms by intersecting them. It is an indication of being insecure. Continuously abstain from holding your arms together before your crotch region, as it shows frailty too. It is known as the Broken Zipper posture. This is one stance that shows weakness and accommodation simultaneously and henceforth, must be maintained a strategic distance.

Try not to continue modifying your sleeve buttons in general public location as it again shows you are a lot of worried about your weaknesses of turning out in broad daylight. The women must make a note that they ought not to grasp their bags near themselves as they talk as it shows their cautious position and their uncertain nature.

Zero Arm Blockage

At the point when you are in an eatery, don't grip your espresso cup away from plain view. There ought to be no arm boundary when you conversing with someone else. Keep open non-verbal communication and hold the espresso cup aside.

Use the Parallel Over Perpendicular

In bunch talks, it is a command that when you need to point towards somebody, don't utilize the hand that will be opposite to them. Utilize the other arm that can point to them and can be parallel to your chest as well. Having the arm opposite to your chest to indicate out others is commonly an inconsiderate motion. Continuously attempt to have the arms parallel to the body.

Arms and hands must be utilized cautiously in discussions. The development of your arms and hands can make or blemish your exchange and can change the results fundamentally.

Head Action

We use the head, as much as any other part of our body, to communicate actively without using words. There are a few basic head gestures you can learn to recognize and use to express different emotions and thoughts.

The most common one is nodding. In most cases, it is a sign of agreement although it is often culturally bound. For example, people in Bulgaria nod for "No" and you may get confused if you are in a meeting with a representative of this nation.

Nodding often prompts your counterpart to talk more because you are sending them signals of agreement. During a meeting, the more you nod, the better and more relaxed a person would feel because you express agreement with their statement and are of the same opinion. You show support. However, don't overdo it because you risk looking funny.

On the other hand, head-shaking is considered a refusal, a literal "No". In business body language, shaking your head would mean you do not like the proposal being made. You may come up with a counter-proposal or refuse the deal altogether. If you see your counterpart shaking his head during your speech, change the direction of the conversation and try to understand their intentions and meet halfway.

Leaning forward or tilting your head to the side can mean that you are listening carefully and/or are focused on what the other person is saying.

During meetings or in your personal life you may see a person scratching their head. This may mean that they are trying to remember something, or feel uncertain. It may even mean lying. However, you must always be careful to watch for other gestures to support your opinion because scratching can be purely physiological – the person may have dandruff or is just sweating.

More often than not, head gestures and positions are tied to gestures with hand or the position of the body and facial expressions in the so-called clusters that map to interest or boredom, for example.

One of the gestures that most authors advise us to avoid is touching your face during meetings or dates. In most cases, this means that you are either lying or you feel insecure. Such gestures are often involuntary, but you can exercise at home and try not to use them. If you cover your mouth during a meeting, it will signal your partner that you are lying. The same applies if you touch your nose or rub your eyes.

Some simple rules to follow include the following:

Covering Your Mouth – you can cough, this way camouflaging the real gesture;

Touching Your Nose – if your hand or fingers involuntarily go towards your nose, you can either stop and put your hand under your chin and lean forward to show investment in the discussion or just run your fingers through your hair. It may show nervousness or confidence depending on your facial expression and the tone of your voice;

Rubbing Your Eyes – try instead to stop right before you have reached your eye and turn the gesture into one of interest – support your head with your palm rested on one of your cheeks and your index finger pointing up. This shows interest and assessment.

All of these are effective when you are listening. In case you are the speaker, try to avoid them altogether.

Not all gestures like touching your face or head are negative. As mentioned above, resting your palm on your cheek with your index finger pointing up means you are interested in the conversation and listening carefully while assessing the situation. However, the moment you start supporting your head with all fingers, it signals boredom.

Women often use hair-flip or hair-toss unconsciously to show they are attracted to a man. In a business environment, the hair-toss may mean that the woman feels confident about herself. In rare cases, when the hair-toss is preceded by touching or playing with her hair, it may mean nervousness or insecurity. Therefore, during business meetings, it is best to avoid touching your hair. A piece of advice – if you have noticed that you touch your hair often, go to the meeting with your hair tied to avoid unwanted body language signals that may ruin your position.

Another gesture is rubbing your chin. This usually means reflection and is used before you reach a decision. The same applies to rubbing your neck although it may also mean that you cannot make a decision, you are still not convinced.

If you want to exude confidence or even arrogance, you can put both your hands behind your head. This gesture, however, can only be used amongst equals or if you are surrounded by people on lower positions than you. Do not use it in front of your manager or people holding higher positions.

It Is Important to Understand Body Language

Most individuals rely on social networks and texts to connect in the modern digital age, and this is a very reliable way for doing so.

While digital communication enables people to speak at convenience and can reduce stress on certain individuals, something can be lost in so doing, and because you are incapable of recognizing the person when you speak to them, you can miss key non-verbal signs in addition to verbal ones such as vocal inflections. Digital communication has become the main method for people around the world, and to satisfy this, there is the likelihood that body language will proceed to develop. Most of the time you may hear the negatives of body language. Maybe you are told not to twist in a certain way, sit this way or that way. However, body language can influence your life positively. Let us look at what you should do to maximize body language.

Non Verbal Communication

Body language refers to the nonverbal cues they are used for communication. Such nonverbal cues, as per scholars, constitute a major part of your daily interaction. The things we do not say can still express volumes of knowledge from our facial expressions to our physical movements. It was proposed that facial expressions can speak for 60% to 65% of all interactions. It is important to recognize non-verbal communication, but it is also important to listen to other signals such as meaning. In many situations, instead of relying on a single event, you must look at signals as a band. You may be wondering what you should look at as you interpret non-verbal cues. Well, this chapter is going to fully answer your queries and leave you enlightened.

How to Use and Improve Body Language

After getting the tips, you may be asking yourself whether indeed body language influences your life positively. I am here to prove to you that indeed, your life is bound to transform if you take your time to nurture your body language and its relevance in each and everything that you do. You should know what to use where to be organized and articulate. This book will focus on positive body language. That includes; good eye contact, effective engagement, targeted gestures that make your message more understandable and effective. In essence body language has been found to create and enhance your confidence, influence, and all-round success. More studies have revealed that the people who know how to use their body language are more likable, persuasive, competent, and also possess a high level of emotional intelligence. That means that they can command presence and manipulate their way into various platforms and win people's hearts. That also explains the success in negotiation which we shall look at later in the book.

Let us go ahead and look at the ways that body language will transform your life.

Positive non-verbal communication changes your frame of mind. The research found that deliberately changing your non-verbal communication to make it increasingly positive improves your demeanor since it powerfully affects your hormones.

It leads to an increase in testosterone. At the point when you hear of testosterone, your mind can easily be swayed to focus on athletics, yet testosterone's significance covers substantially more than games. Regardless of whether you are a man or a lady, testosterone improves your certainty and makes other individuals consider you to be progressively dependable and positive. Research shows that positive non-verbal communication builds your testosterone levels by 20%.

Body language leads to a reduction of cortisol. Cortisol is a pressure hormone that blocks execution and makes negative wellbeing impacts over the long haul. Reduction of cortisol levels limits pressure and empowers you to think all the more plainly, especially in troublesome and testing circumstances. Research shows that positive non-verbal communication diminishes cortisol levels by 25%.

It makes a ground-breaking blend. While a reduction in cortisol and an increase in testosterone is incredible in its special ways, the two together are a ground-breaking blend that is normally observed among individuals in high positions. This blend makes the certainty and clearness of mind that are perfect for managing tight deadlines, intense choices, and huge amounts of work. Individuals who normally have high testosterone and low levels of cortisol are known to flourish under pressure. Indeed, you can utilize positive non-verbal communication to make yourself like this regardless of whether it doesn't occur normally.

It makes you progressively attractive and likable. During a study in a university, students watched soundless videos of doctors having an interaction with their patients. Just by watching the doctors' non-verbal communication, the students could conclude the doctors wound up getting sued by their patients. Non-verbal communication is an enormous factor by the way you're seen and can be a higher priority than your manner of speaking or even what you state. Figuring out how to utilize constructive use of body language will make individuals have confidence in you, like you and trust you more.

It shows capability. In an investigation, scientists found that a one-second video of candidates in a campaign was able to pinpoint the potential candidate that was voted for. All this because of their body language. While this may not build your confidence in the democratic procedure, it shows that the view of capability has a solid establishment in non-verbal communication.

Body language improves emotional intelligence. Your capacity to viably convey your feelings and thoughts is vital to your passionate knowledge. Individuals whose non-verbal communication is negative have a dangerous, infectious impact on everyone around them. Attempting to improve your non-verbal communication profoundly affects your emotional intelligence.

Public Speaking

The Importance of Public Speaking

Most people cringe at the thought of giving a speech in public however, the spoken word has so much power over written speech. Therefore, whether you are a teacher, student, business owner, employee or leader, public speaking is a very important skill to master and have.

You can be required to make a project presentation at school, make a presentation at work, pitch a product or service to a client or deliver a speech at a family gathering all of which requires you to be conversant and comfortable with public speaking. For those who are not good at it, it is a skill worth learning. Here are some reasons why the skill is important:

Public Speaking Increases Self-Confidence

Our self-esteem, in most cases, centers on what other people think about us, which should not always be the case. Through public speaking, we are able to increase our communication skills and thus become more comfortable around people and talking to them. The better you become at public speaking, it is likely that your self-confidence will only increase and this will, in turn, make you an even better public speaker.

It Increases Knowledge

Event organizers do not ask just anyone in the crowd that is interested in delivering a speech to stand up and do it. Before a public speaker stands up in front of a crowd to deliver a speech, he or she must do research. Therefore,

103

over a long time, a person is bound to improve his or her research skills and gather an immense amount of knowledge. The preparation process also helps the speaker to understand the topic even better.

It Is an Opportunity to Show and Share Knowledge

When a speaker is standing to speak in front of a group of people, he or she is transferring information from him or herself to the audience in attendance. Therefore, taking up speaking roles positions an individual as an expert with knowledge in a particular area. People in the audience will, therefore, look up to a speaker not just with regard to the content he or she is sharing, but also with all the aspects surrounding the topic he or she is sharing on.

Public Speaking Delivers a Message to a Larger Audience over a Short Period

Speeches allow speakers to deliver one message to a large number of people over a short period. It would take a very long time for all the people in the audience to get down, conduct the same research, and come up with the same or even similar findings. Furthermore, the audience at an event where a speaker is giving a speech can also play the role of spreading the message to other people they know that could not make it to the event.

It Provides a Platform for Advocating for Certain Causes

If an individual has a certain cause that he or she holds dear, he or she can make it known to other people by holding public speeches and telling people about it. Some of the greatest revolutions in the past have gained massive followings after expert orators have charged people up with their speeches. People who deliver speeches in a great way convince their listeners to buy into the cause and in the process lead to positive social change.

It Brings People Together

Speeches foster cohesion because they present an opportunity for people to come together to share ideas. Politicians running for public office always call their supporters together to listen to them speak, and the more they address big crowds the better they become at delivering speeches and the more people want to vote for them. Such a public gathering will force human beings to interact with other like-minded people, and these interactions can foster the development of a community.

It Helps Develop Other Skills

Public speaking not only improves the speaker's communication skills but also helps to develop other skills in them such as leadership, negotiation skills, and people skills. You might discover that the people who are the greatest public speakers end up making some of the best leaders because of the leadership and interpersonal skills they develop in their quest to becoming expert public speakers.

Public Speaking Advances You in Life

Public speaking makes you more noticeable and can, therefore, fast track you to a promotion. Public speaking puts you in a position of influence, which means you can make a difference in your workplace and community. With this skill, you can negotiate for a job and better terms. Business owners with good public speaking abilities can also close deals quickly.

Principles ofPublic Speaking

As mentioned earlier, public speaking is the process of standing in front of a crowd and relaying information. Public speaking is not as easy as many would think and most people who are good at it have received training, or have done it so many times. Here are a few guidelines on the foundations of public speaking and the steps an individual can take to become better at it.

The principles of public speaking include:

1. Perfection - It is almost impossible to speak in public and not making any mistakes, even the gurus of public speaking sometimes make mistakes. You can stutter, misspeak or find yourself saying a couple of "umms" which make you sound less confident. However, when you make a mistake no one actually knows or cares but you. Therefore, keep going, only apologize if the mistake was momentous. If anything, the audience relates to you more when you make a mistake because it shows that no one is perfect.

2. Perception - Every day we hold routine conversations with people either at work or at home and we do it by being ourselves. However, when it comes to public speaking, something changes. We forget about being ourselves and concentrate on the public. Public speaking is all about being relaxed, holding an interesting conversation and being comfortable but most importantly being ourselves. Do not try to change the process through which you arrange your thoughts and how you normally speak just because you are addressing more people than you normally do.

3. Visualization - Visualization is key in public speaking. Practicing and creating images and technique in your

mind can help you communicate the message. It is also a good way to get rid of panic and anxiety when speaking in public. You can also visualize the audience applauding at the end to keep you motivated.

4. Discipline - In order to be an effective public speaker, you have to keep practicing. Practice makes perfect or in this case efficient. Someone who has been speaking in public for years will be more efficient than the one just starting out. Even the best musicians in the world, have to practice every day. Even if they have been singing for years, they still need to practice in order to sound good on stage.

5. Personalize the Message - It is important to tailor your message to the audience. When you generalize, the audience has no way of relating to the message and may even stop paying attention. The audience usually relates to you more and even warm-ups to you when you personalize the message and share your own personal experiences. People like to hear about other people's victories and tragedies because they have probably gone through the same thing.

6. Inspiration - A good twist to public speaking is to take the focus off yourself and shift it to your audience. After all, your message is supposed to benefit them and not you per se. When creating your speech know the end purpose and always have the audience in mind. Keep the focus on the audience, look at their reactions and adjust your speech accordingly. You can even engage them while speaking.

7. Anticipation - When speaking in public, avoid making long boring speeches. People tend to drift away when the speeches are too long and wonder what you have just told when it is too short. Always make it shorter than anticipated and leave them wanting more. Leave the

audience wishing that you had spoken a little more. It means they enjoyed every bit of the speech.

8. Authenticity - Authenticity is vital. When speaking in public you are only as good as your speech. Great speeches do not just happen; the best ones are perfect for the person who makes them. Your speech should have something that makes it unique to only you. The audience prefers listening to a speaker who connects with them personally and emotionally than the one who is just blunt and gives a great speech.

9. Authority - When you are on that stage or platform, you are in charge. Speaking in public is already an act of leadership and therefore you should ensure you are guiding the audience. When you lose your authority while on stage, the audience will stop listening to you. Being in authority, however, does not mean you cannot be vulnerable or share your mistakes.

10. The Purpose of Your Speech - Before you make a speech, you need to know the basic purpose of the speech you are about to give. There are three general reasons why people give speeches:

- To inform, you want to pass on some information to the audience that they do not currently have.
- To entertain, you want to keep the audience lively and laughing. This kind of speech sometimes may contain important information but delivered in an amusing manner
- To persuade, you want to change the audience's opinions or perceptions about something.

Know Your Audience

A good way to better your public speaking skills is to speak to familiar faces. If you do not have friends or people, you know there, talk to one or two people in the audience when you arrive. They become your allies in the audience. As you speak, it is also important to watch for feedback and adjust your speech accordingly. At the same time, when you speak, ensure that your speech moves people to action, if that is never the case, then it will have zero effect.

Capture Their Attention

You have to be relaxed when speaking in public, so avoid arriving late and rushing to the stage without giving yourself time to relax. Start with a personal story or quote, it is a good way to capture the audience attention and calm your nerves.

Strategies: How to Talk in Public with Confidence and Overcome the Fear

Here are a few tips on how you can start your journey to overcoming glossophobia:

Research on Your Topic

The trick to giving good speeches is to prepare well for them at least a week before the actual day you will stand to deliver them. This means getting as much information as you can about your topic and understanding it so that you are confident enough to present your material and to answer any questions that may come up. Knowing your topic also enables you to engage better with the audience in case a discussion arises. If you can, anticipate some of the questions the audience might ask and come up with answers.

Practice Makes Perfect

Once you have your speech drafted out, practice it as much as you can because the more you practice the better you will become. Do it in front of a mirror or in front of your pets if you have to since doing so will help you to visualize how you will feel on a material day. Ask a few family members or friends to listen to it and give you feedback. You can also practice in front of complete strangers who will not mind listening to you. Giving frequent motivational speeches at local groups can also improve your public speaking skills.

Give Shorter Speeches at First

Overcoming glossophobia might take some time, though it is always different in different people. More often than not, this process requires individuals to take baby steps to overcome it. With this in mind, you should try giving shorter speeches before you move to longer ones. A good way to practice this is to open the podium for another speaker. Knowing that you are not the main attraction will somehow put you at ease. Such speeches should also not go longer than three minutes.

Give Your Speech in Familiar Locations

If you have to give a speech and you happen to have a say in where your presentation will take place, choose a place that you are familiar with. For example, if you are supposed to give a business presentation choose to do it in your conference room, which you are familiar with. This way you are aware of the sitting capacity, the sitting arrangement, the lighting and the section of the room to plug in your electronics for the presentation. Doing this also removes the stress of setting up and the risk of something going wrong or not working.

Engage the Audience

Engaging with the audience can help make you less nervous. There are a number of ways you can do this; you can great a few of the people who come in before the presentation starts, you can start the presentation by asking your audience a question or you can invite the audience to comment on a few points in your speech. Doing this gives you an opportunity to take a break and reorganize your thoughts as well as to give your audience an opportunity to open up to you as well.

Be Vulnerable

Depending on the crowd you are addressing, you can get real with the audience and admit to them that you are nervous or have forgotten what you wanted to say. Chances are the audience will laugh when you say such things and this will put you at ease. It is also okay to request a minute to recompose yourself.

Use Props

Props can be anything from a video, to a PowerPoint presentation, to another speaker, to a person in the audience who can help you read points on the screen. If you are nervous about speaking, using props lessens the time you have to speak. Audience activities, a question, and a discussion session take the attention away from you.

Darken the Room

If your audience's sharp stares and stern faces make you nervous, forget about imagining them in their undies and dim the lights. If you must give an excuse for doing so pretend that you cannot read the screen properly with all the glare from the lights. This way you are less distracted and intimidated by people's facial expressions that can focus on

111

delivering your speech. However, this mostly works if there is a stage and the lighting is separate.

Breathe

It is normal for people to speed through their speeches when nervous. Reading a speech at lightning speed will sure not help in keeping you calm. Improper breathing can affect your speech and make you sound out of breath or less confident. Instead, you should strategically pause in between sentences or engage the audience in an activity so that you can catch your breath and take a sip of water.

Celebrate the Success

Once you have gotten through what might have been the biggest challenge of your life, reflect on how you performed. You can ask a friend to sit through your speech or ask them to record the speech and then review it later. Applaud yourself for the parts that went well and polish up on the areas that need improving. With time, you will master the art of public speaking.

Manage Shyness

The ability to maintain a good pattern of conversation skills is one of the many reasons why we are tagged as humans. It is often said that humans are social beings; however, how does one buttress this obvious fact if one does not know how best to maintain a conversation with anyone?

One of the many rules of communication with anyone is said to be the fact that the decoder has to understand the encoder in other that communication is made perfect.

While this is the case, this might prove a lot of difficulty to a lot of people who are shy, because they feel that people

112

might see the flaws in them and major on them. This leads us to the question of, "why do some humans feel shy?"

WHY DO PEOPLE FEEL SHY?

A lot of people feel shy for a number of reasons, more often than not, it is said that the major reason why a lot of people feel shy is because they have the low self-esteem, while this might be true, there are a plethora of reasons why people would feel shy, and it does not necessarily have to be because they have a low self-esteem about themselves.

In a recent survey which has been conducted on a set of shy people, as regards the reasons why they are shy when communicating with people within their social setting, we were able to outline some reasons why people are shy, and they include:

Private Upbringing:

Some people are shy because of the way that they were brought up. It would be interesting to know that some people were brought up by their parents in such a way that they do not interact with people on the outside, and this is owing to a lot of reasons.

The major being the fact that they do not want their wards to make friends with bad companies, and this ends up making them feel like they need to have their lives in private. For such kind of kids, when they eventually have the need to go outside of their home, they might have a reason or two to hold back and not communicate with the people that they find within their social setting.

Social Factors:

There are a lot of things that could contribute to the social factor, which makes a lot of people shy. One of such reasons is because of one thing or the other that such people have been made to come in contact with.

A lot of people become shy because of a desire that they had which made them disappointed or because they were turned down by someone that they admire. All of these a part of the social factors that could make people shy

Fear:

Some people also become shy because they are scared of being under the spotlight or being seen by people. There are tons of people who become shy because they are scared of what people might think of them, but they also fail to understand that regardless of wherever it is that you are, you would always attract some kind of attention to yourself.

Validation:

A lot of people are shy because they do not get validations from those that they expect it from. They presume that the only way that they can know that they are doing things the right way is when people acknowledge them for doing it that way, they do not realize that a lot more people feel the need to do the right things because it appeals well enough to their conscience.

Kindly note: Whether a person is shy or not, there would always be consequences for one's actions or inactions. Regardless of this fact, one must strive at every point in his or her life to make sure that they are in the best part of whatever it is that they do.

CONSEQUENCES OF BEING A SHY PERSON

Many people might say that it is okay to be a shy person, especially because it allows you to be at the safe side of things, but in more ways than one, being shy could cost you a whole lot, and this leads us to some of the consequences of being shy. To mention but a few of those consequences would include:

When You Are Shy, It Gives the Wrong Impression of You:

There are people in the world that we live in today that didn't mean to give the impression that they gave to others, but because they are receptive and shy, they gave those impressions.

One of those impressions is the fact that people would assume that you are proud, just because you are a shy person, and such kind of impression would have been easily refuted if you are the kind that is vocal about their intents. Nobody really wants to be involved with one that they assume to be proud, and this leads us to the next consequence of being shy.

When You Are Shy, People Will Not Approach You for Something That They Feel That You Can Do:

Research has it that people that are shy are those that seldom talk about their abilities. When people do not know that you are capable of doing something, you don't get the best of your relationship with people, whether it is official, social, or any other kind of relationship.

When You Are Shy, You Are Bound to Be Stagnant:

When you are shy, you are bound to be stagnant because you do not know how best to express yourself so much that you can bring people to find interest in the work that you do. Many people who are shy are always people who are multi-talented, but they do not make the best of their skills because they chose to be mum when they could easily have spoken their minds about a particular situation.

115

You Can Be Cheated:

People who are shy are people who can be easily cheated because people assume that regardless of whatever it is that they do to such people, they would never talk or complain about them.

There is nothing to be admired about a shy person, and this is what leads us to our next topic.

How to Talk to Anyone

Relationships Talk

T he foundation of all human relationships is how well you can bond with another person. Two people start off as strangers, and how do they form a bond from there? They start communicating. They interact, they start talking and start getting to know one another and slowly, a relationship begins to form, and it begins with being able to communicate effectively with one another.

Confidence and Have Great Success in Relationships

It is one thing to be confident, and quite another to show it. Can the listeners tell that you're confident? That will inform their expectations. There are those speakers that make a poor first impression and are dismissed from the start. You can see it in the demeanor of the listeners. They sink back into their chairs and look bored. Such a speaker will have a hard time salvaging the situation.

How people perceive you affect how you behave. If the listeners sit up and look eager when you begin to speak, you'll feel energized to do just that. Once you portray confidence from the onset, you raise the expectation, and that perception bounces right back to you.

Enjoy yourself as well. Be excited about the opportunity to speak and the topic at hand. Speak with enthusiasm. Smile. Once you radiate these traits, the crowd will follow suit to the end. Make sure that you have some actionable points at the end, something the listeners can go try out on their own.

Strategies of How to Talk at Work with Confidence and to Have Success

Effective communication is essential in any setting where people come into contact with one another, but in the workplace, it is even more important as it is a major factor in determining the success of the organization. Success in business refers to having an organized team working to attain the organizational goals, meeting production targets, keeping costs of production down, having healthy in-house relationships, and relating well with customers. Securing a market share is also part of business success, and it is a result of all systems working together well, often because people are communicating properly.

Other benefits derived from good communication include:

- Makes employees more engaged: Communication connects persons in the organization towards a single purpose and goal. If the goal is clear, employees understand what they must do to reach the goal.
- Causes the workforce to be more productive: Communication is a key contributor towards the productivity of the workforce because it promotes an understanding of each member's skills and talents, and encourages creativity and innovation. Hence, the organizational planning is done in consideration of each employee's points of excellence. If the results are all excellent, then the company and its workforce will be productive.
- Prevents misunderstandings with the clients: With excellent communication, the needs and preferences of the clients will be clear, the customer will feel heard and understood, new information will be presented in a form

that all parties can understand, and existing conflicts can be straightened out quickly.

- Alleviates conflict: Misunderstandings, feeling disregarded and misunderstood often result in conflict. People also conflict when they fail to understand how others communicate.

How to Resolve Conflicts

Below is a step-by-step tool to help you resolve conflicts that come up at the workplace, and in other forums that involve interaction with people.

Do Not Burry The Conflict

When conflicts arise, do not assume that they didn't happen, or burry them to avoid talking about them. Unresolved issues are ticking time-bombs that build up pressure, and the situation only gets worse with time. Therefore, conflicts should be dealt with as soon as they occur so that there are no problems or hurt feelings as people perform their duties at work.

Speak With The Other Person

Reach out to the other party and let him or her know that you are interested in speaking about the problem. Invite them to choose a time and place that you would conveniently meet to discuss what happened. Ensure that the location has minimal interruptions, if any so that you have ample time to speak and iron out your issues.

Listen

Listening is quite essential because it allows you to see the issue from the other party's perspective. Therefore, listen to what the other party is saying, and get ready to react. Do not interrupt him. Once he is done talking, summarize and rephrase what he said to seek confirmation, so that you are sure that you understood all that was said. Where you need clarifying, ask questions.

Take Note Of The Points Of Agreement And Disagreement

With the other party's help, take note of the issues you agree or disagree on. At the end of it, ask the person to confirm your assessment. Ensure that both parties agree on the areas of conflict that need working on.

Discuss Behavior Not Individuals

As you try to figure out the causes of conflict, it is easy to start attacking each other's personalities. Some people say, "I do not like it when you leave papers containing sensitive information on top of your desk when you are out." Instead, say, "When papers containing sensitive information are left lying on a desk without supervision, the company stands to expose our clients' personal information, and we could wind up with a lawsuit." The first statement addresses the weaknesses of the person, while the second statement attacks the deed itself.

Develop A List Of Priority

Decide on the issues that are of greater significance, and purpose to work on them first before you move on to those of lower consequence. As you start to discuss the issue, let your focus be the future of the company, and how you should work with one another to actualize company goals.

Follow Through With The Plan

Stick to the list of conflict areas, addressing them one-by-one until you get to the end. Ensure that you come to a consensus on the solution to a particular issue before you move on to the next. Through it all, maintain a collaborative attitude so that you remain united, focused, and committed to working out your conflicts.

Forgive Quickly

When conflicts are resolved, the natural thing is to acknowledge that feelings were hurt, assumptions were made, and ignorant words were said. Acknowledge also that your perspective was wrong (if it was), and thank the other party for helping you see from a new perspective. Tell the person that you are sorry, and forgive the person too. Superficial forgiveness is not good enough because it causes grudges that worsen with time, and undermine every progress you had made.

How to Increase Your Self-Esteem

Self-confidence shows in the way you speak. You either have it or you don't; and it shows. People flock to those who are steadfast, while they tend to shy away from those who are weak. If you don't have it, then get it. Yes, it's that easy. You hold the key. You are in charge if you chose to be. Here are some great things you can do to boost your self-confidence:

- Make a conscious decision RIGHT NOW to become self-confident.
- Change what you don't like about yourself. If you think you are rude, work at being a nicer, more considerate person. If you don't like your looks, do what you can to improve them and also determine to focus on inner-beauty as well.
- Make a daily list of ten things you like about yourself. Grab a pen and paper and start RIGHT NOW!
- Ask a trusted friend 10 things they like about you.

- Every day, recall 10 things you have done successfully.
- Praise yourself for every step you take forward.
- Treat yourself to rewards like a special coffee, a good read or a long soak in the tub.
- Verbally tell yourself in the mirror that you are a good and worthy person.
- Forgive yourself for shortcomings.
- Know that you are as good as everyone else

OK, so, if you truly do the steps above, you are well on your way in becoming more confident. You will begin to see yourself in a whole new light and others will see you the same way. You will learn to respect yourself more and others will follow. As the famous psychiatrist and television talk show host, Dr. Phil McGraw says, "You teach people how to treat you." It's true. You are in the driver's seat.

Conclusion

Effective communication is an essential skill that is critical for individuals to learn and master. While it may seem like a daunting task, it is important to remember that even the most successful communicators were not born with this skill; they trained and practiced it. From historical and spiritual leaders to politicians, dictators, and successful spies, the best teachers, legendary seducers, beloved celebrities, business leaders, good parents, popular YouTubers, writers, journalists, psychotherapists, stand-up comedians, and actors, all have honed their communication skills over time. It is my sincere hope that this book has helped bring you closer to achieving effective communication, and has inspired you to continue practicing and improving this essential skill.

I wish you the best of luck on your journey and hope you get there soon! It's important to remember that the people you surround yourself with have an influence on you, so start connecting with others who also want to become better communicators. Consider joining a Toastmasters or rhetoric group, practice speaking in front of a mirror and camera, read books about social psychology and body language, and never stop learning. The reward for your hard work will be worth it! I have faith in you!

*** BONUS 2 ***

As promised, I am happy to announce Bonus 2 "Time Management, Problem Solving and Critical Thinking."

These strategies will help you better manage your time and solve problems more efficiently. In addition, critical thinking is an essential skill that can help people make informed decisions.

What you learn will be very useful in both your personal and work life and can help you break out of the circle of overthinking. Studying these skills can help you develop greater awareness, save time, and be more productive. Follow us on this journey and discover how these skills can help you achieve success.

Have a great read!

https://BookHip.com/NWVFJJQ

Made in the USA
Coppell, TX
01 February 2024

28486375R00070